This Book Belongs To:

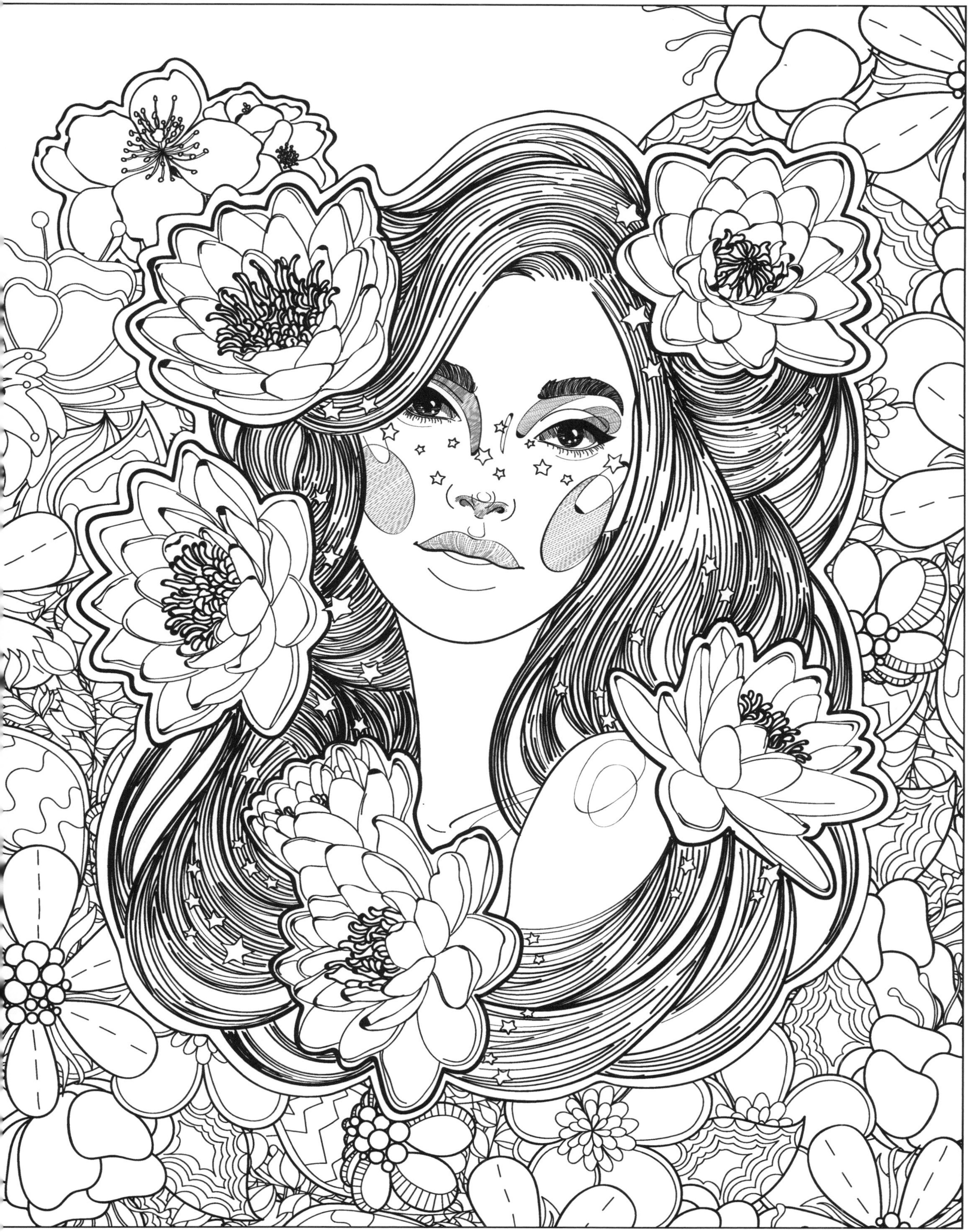

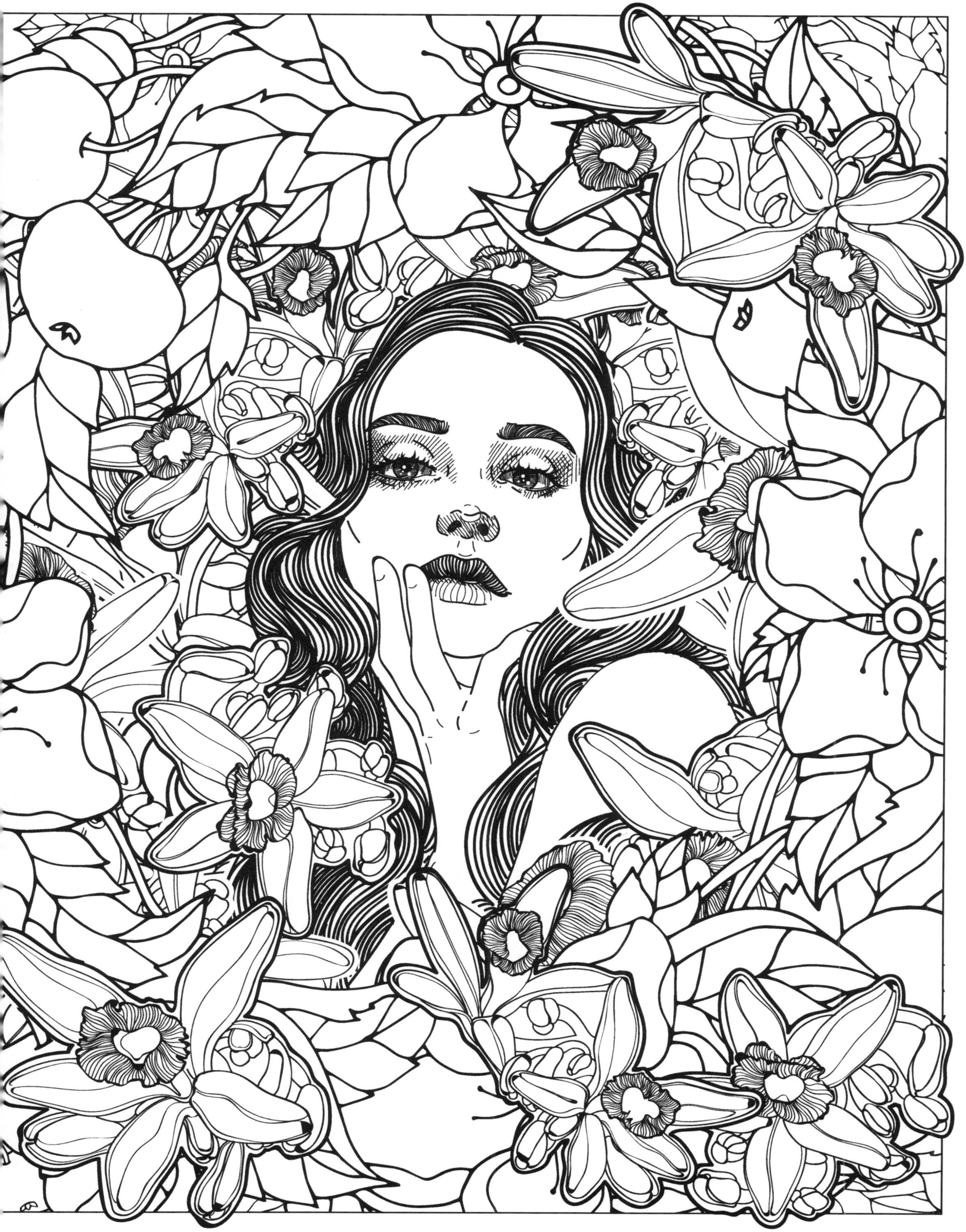

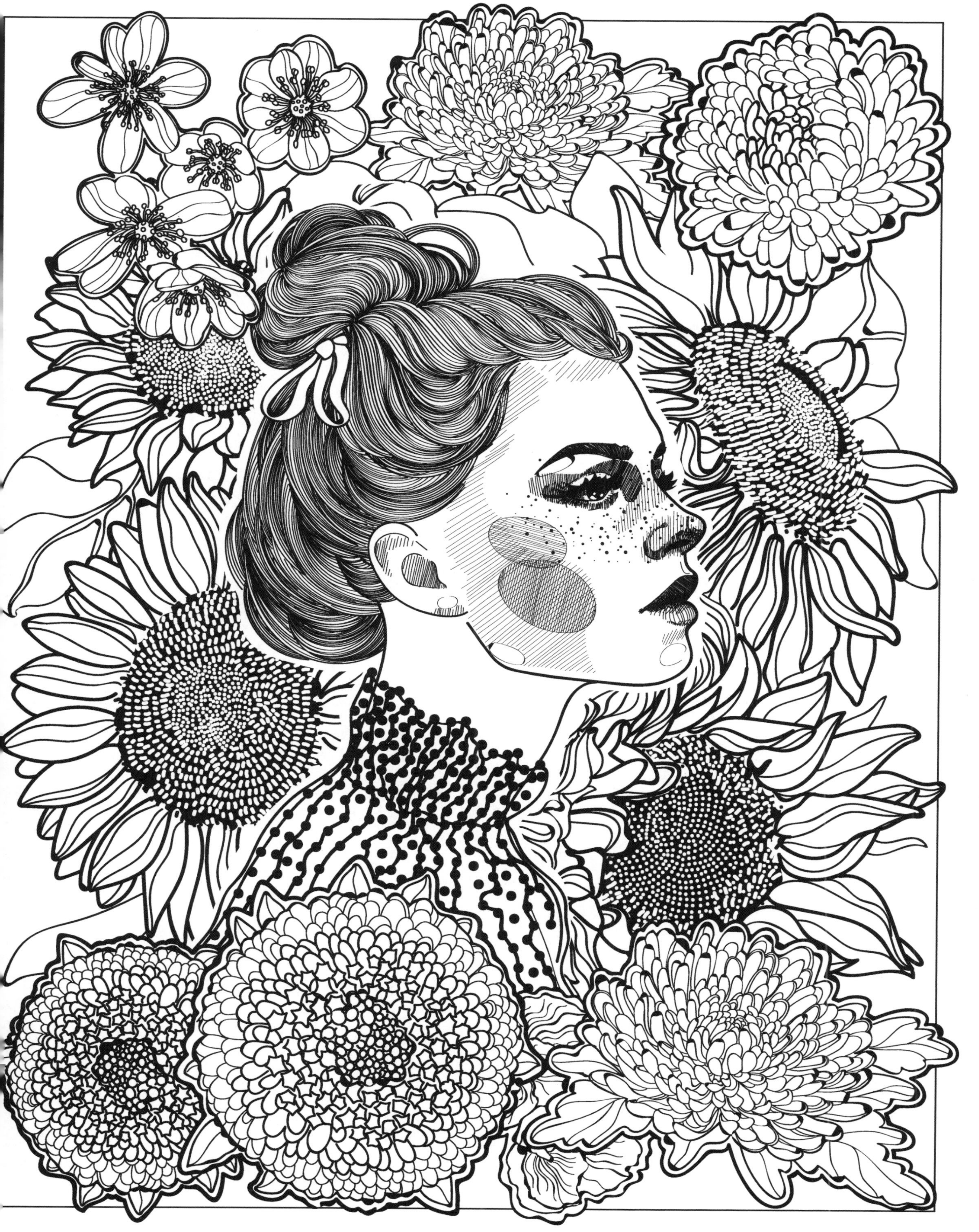

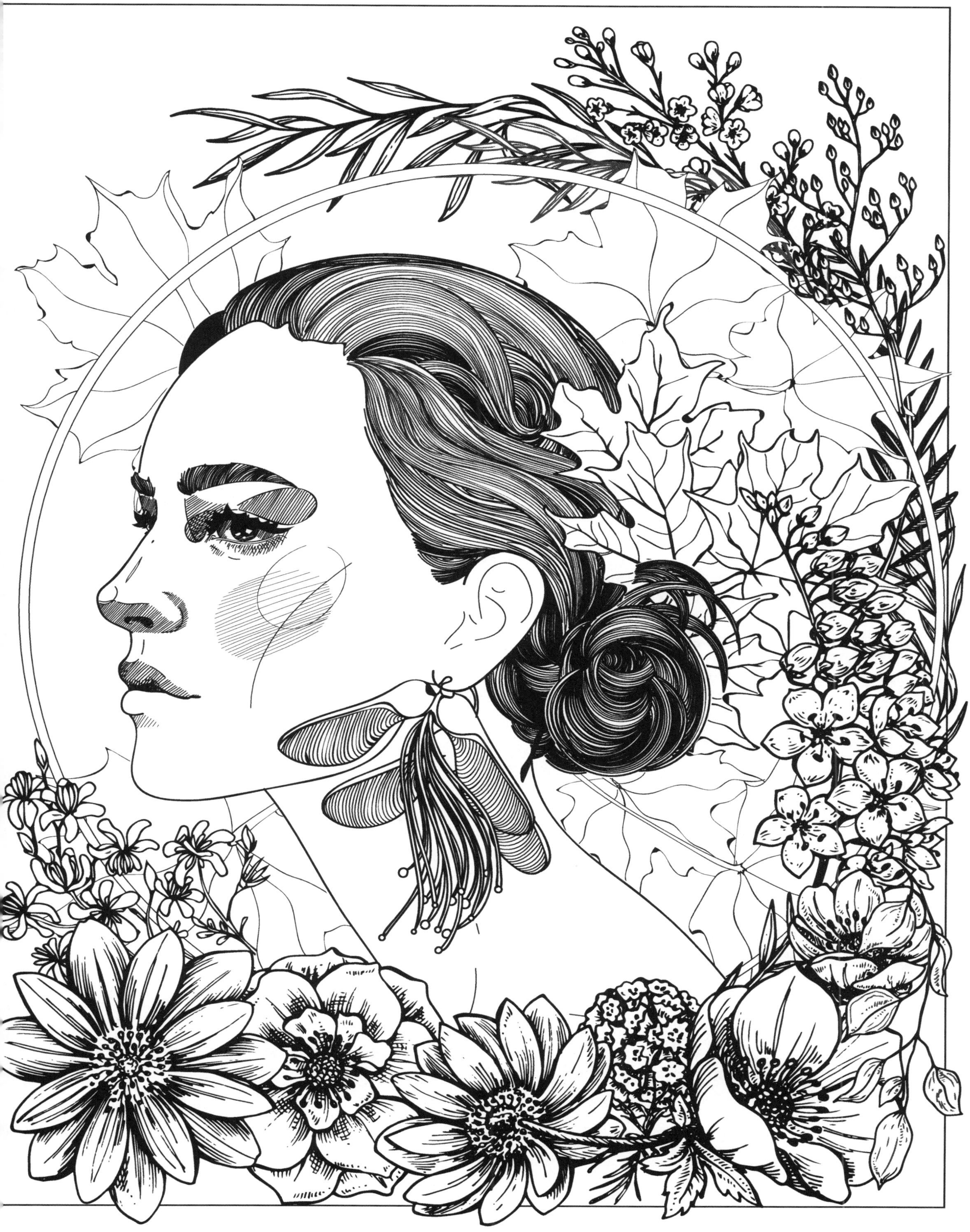

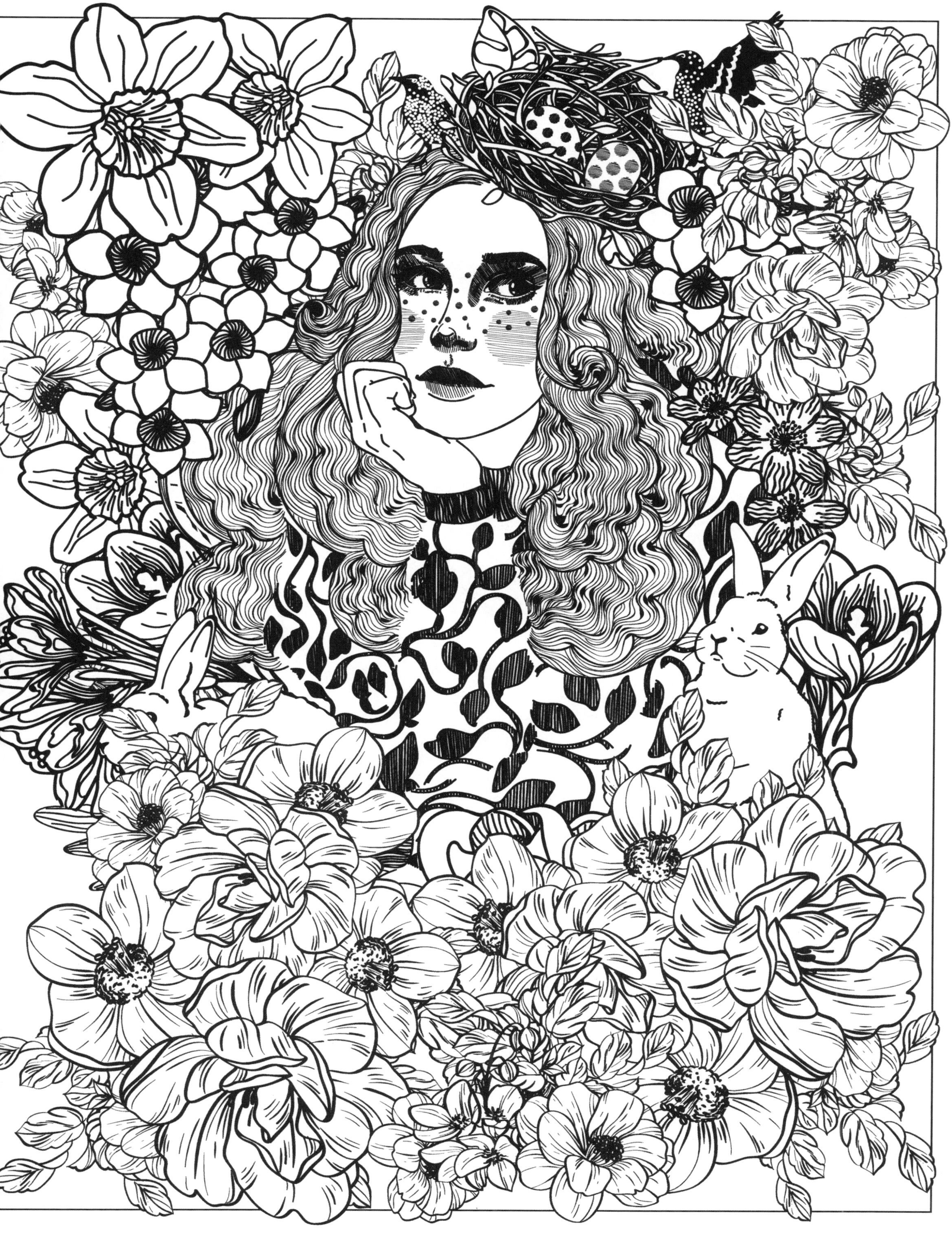

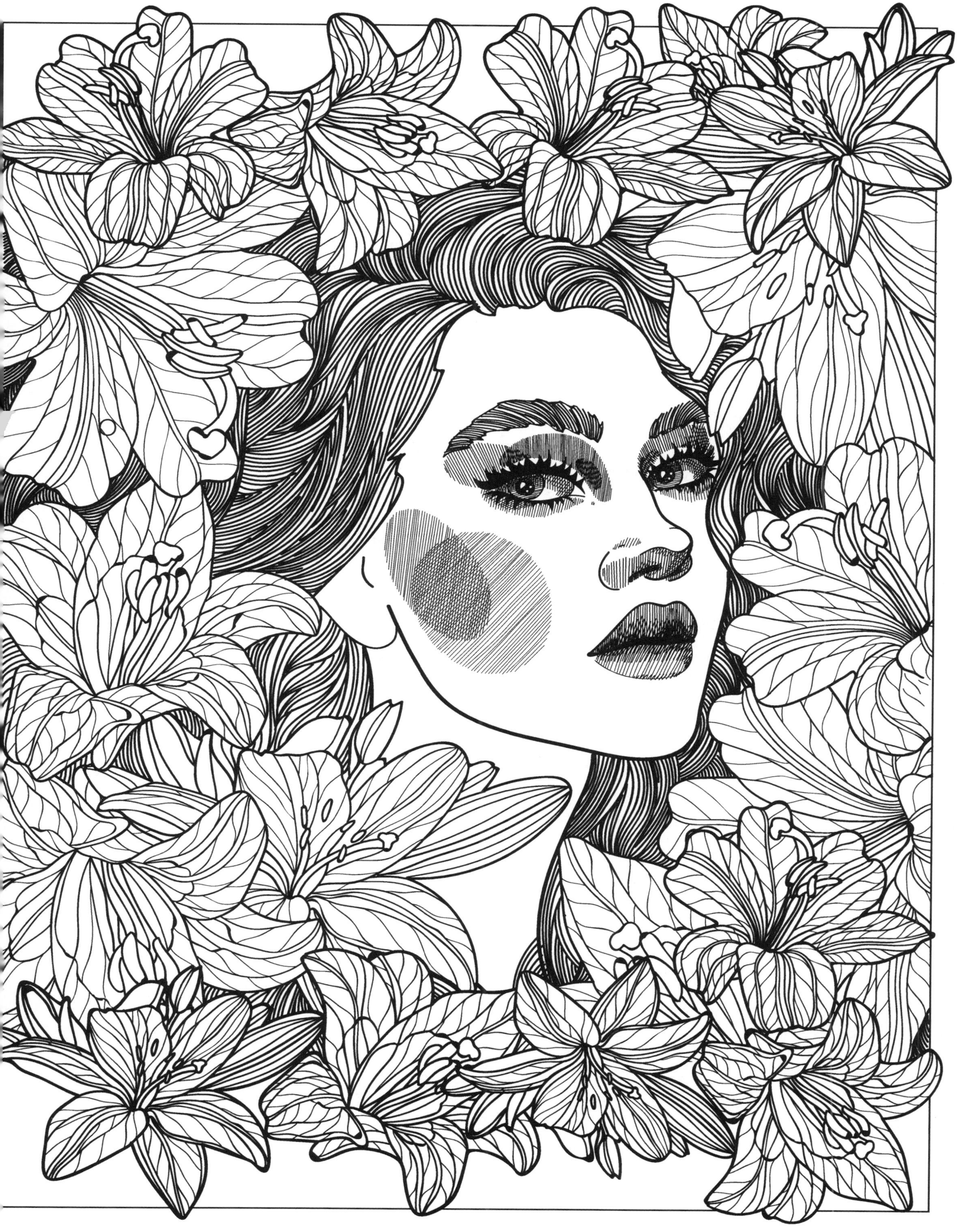

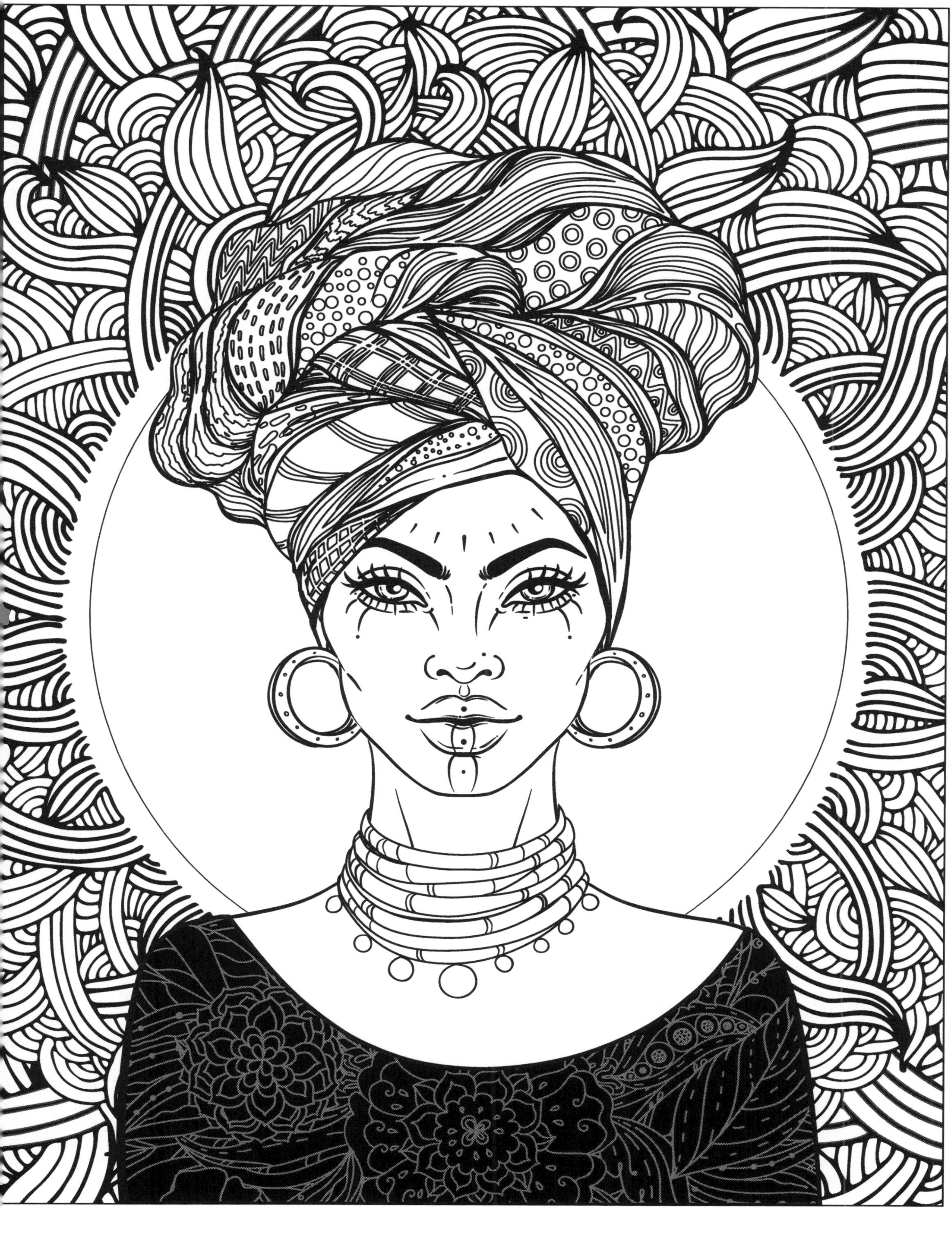

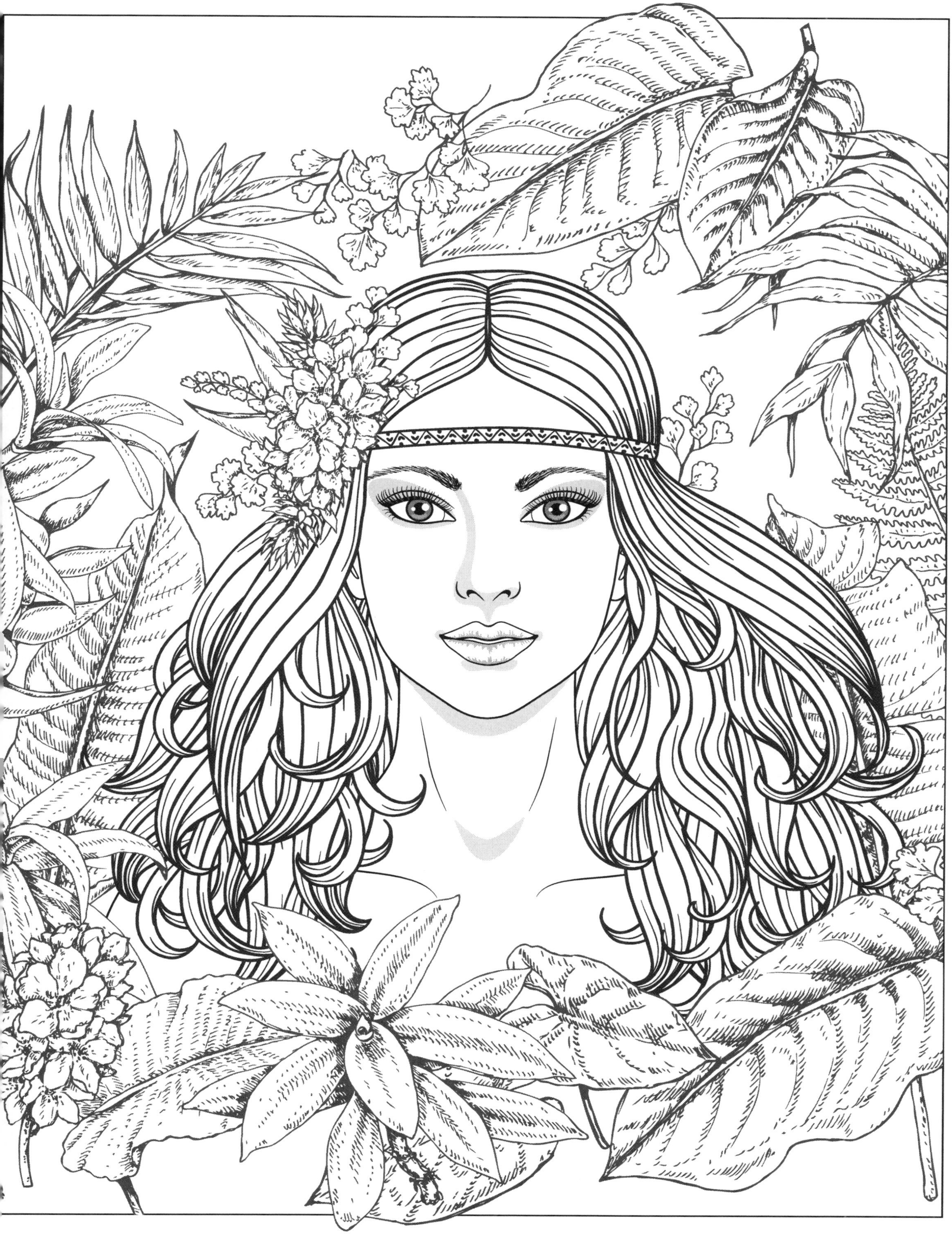

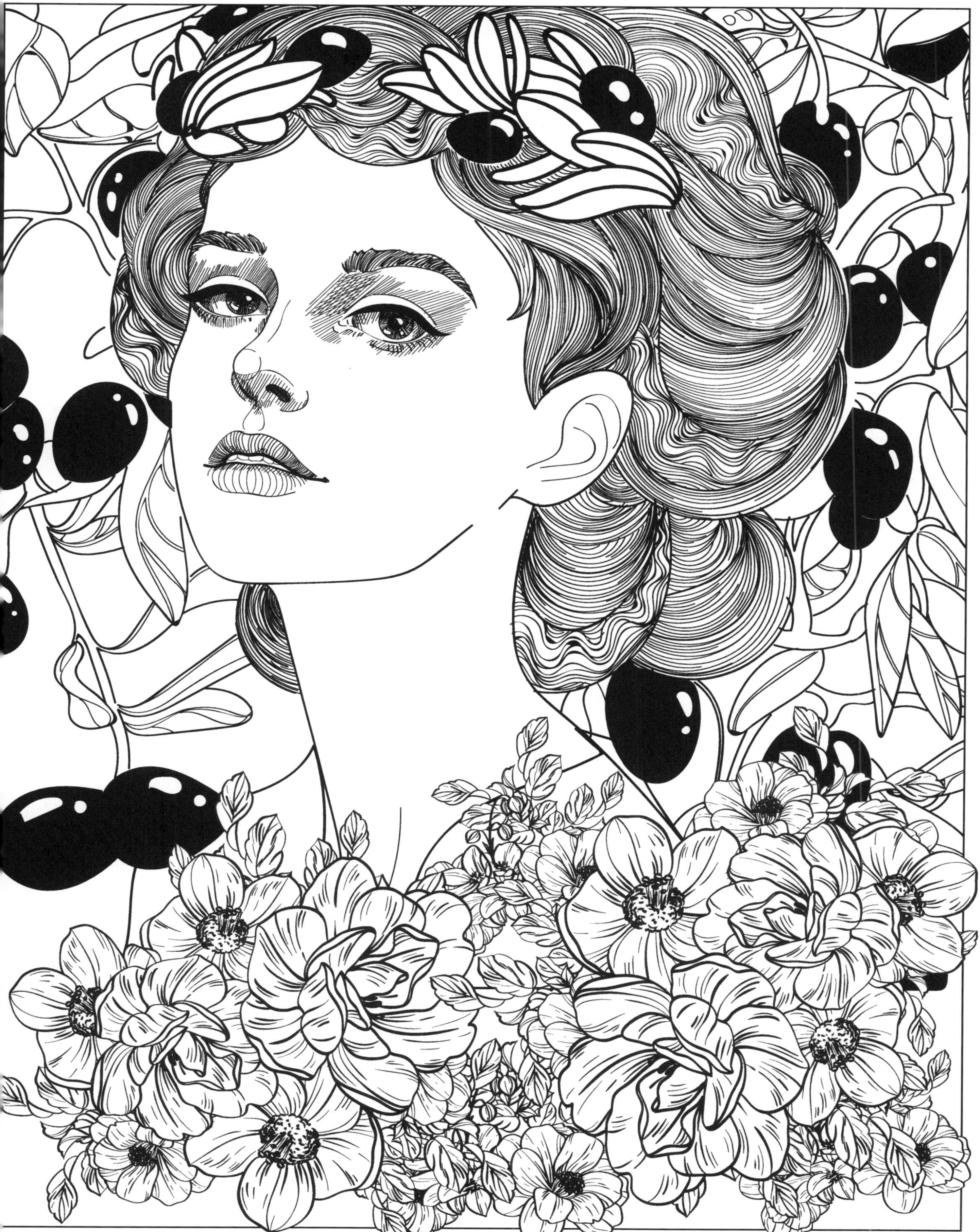

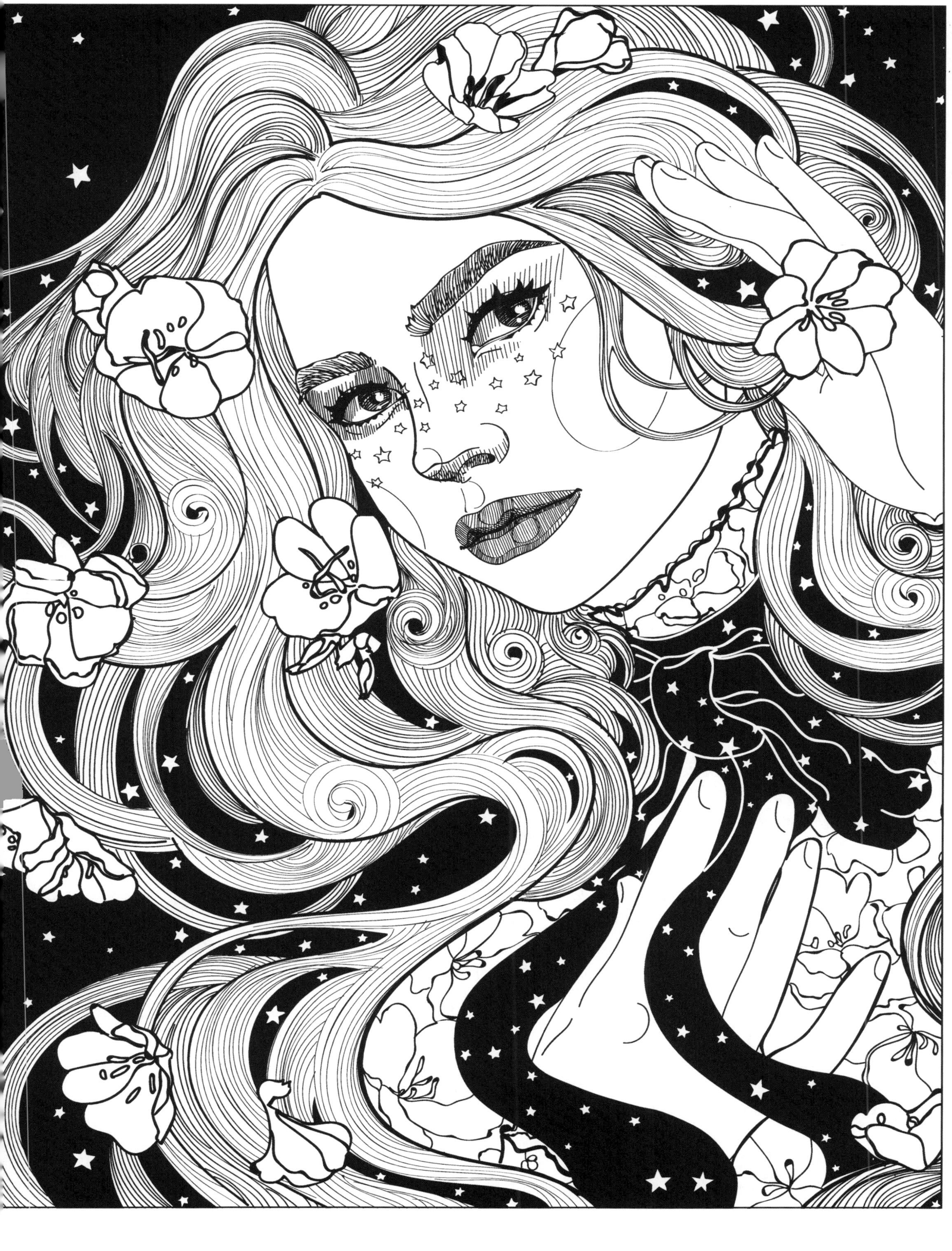

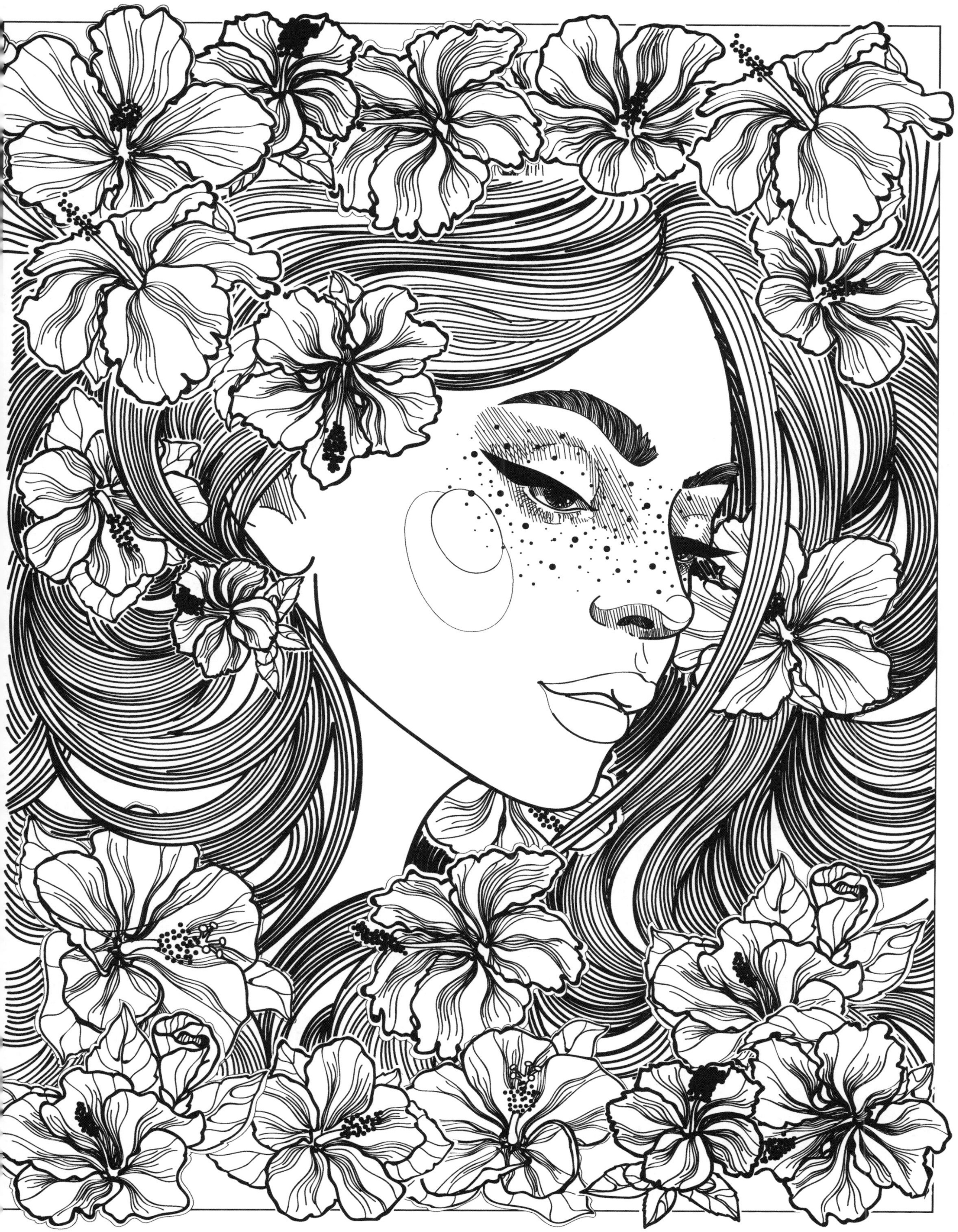

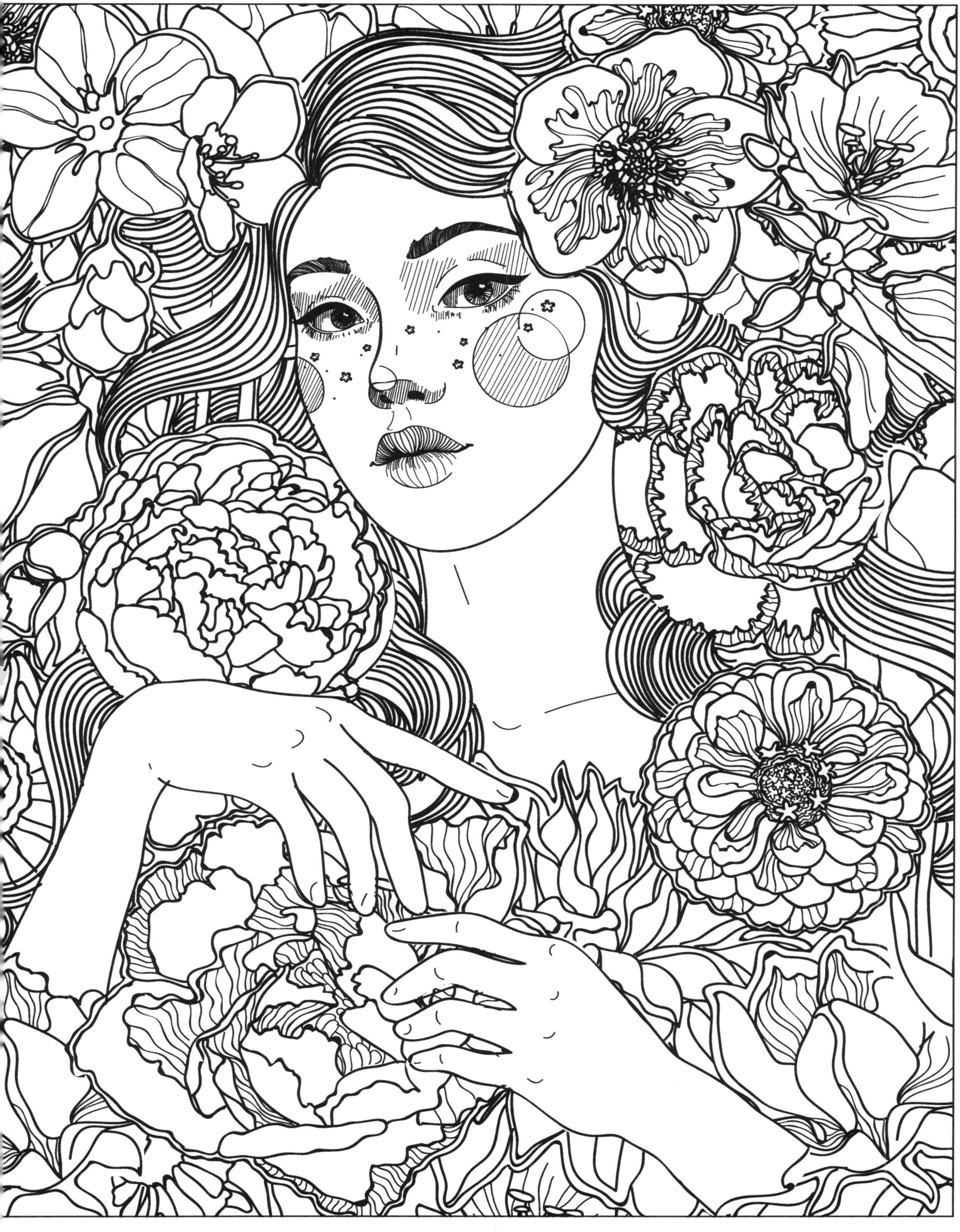

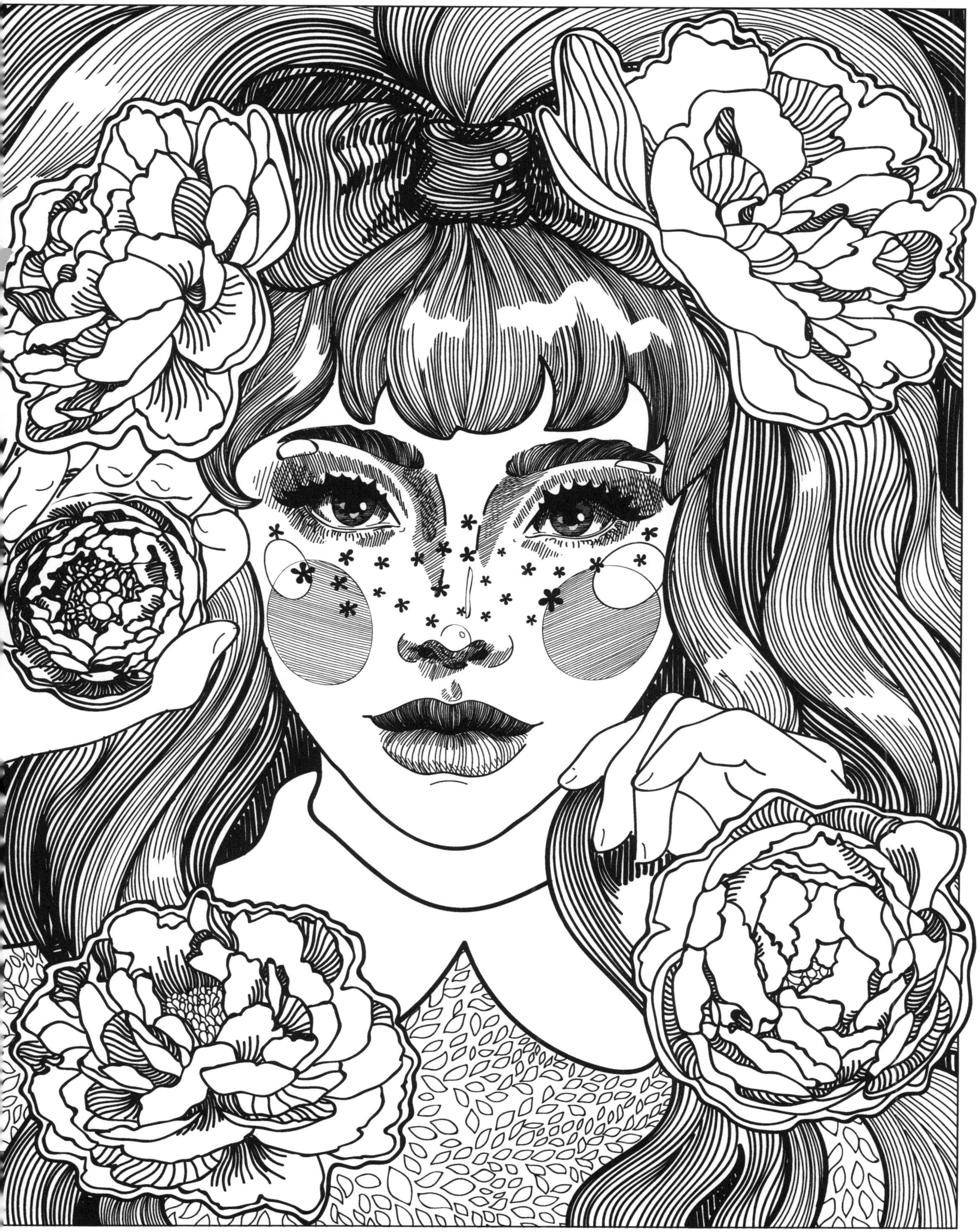

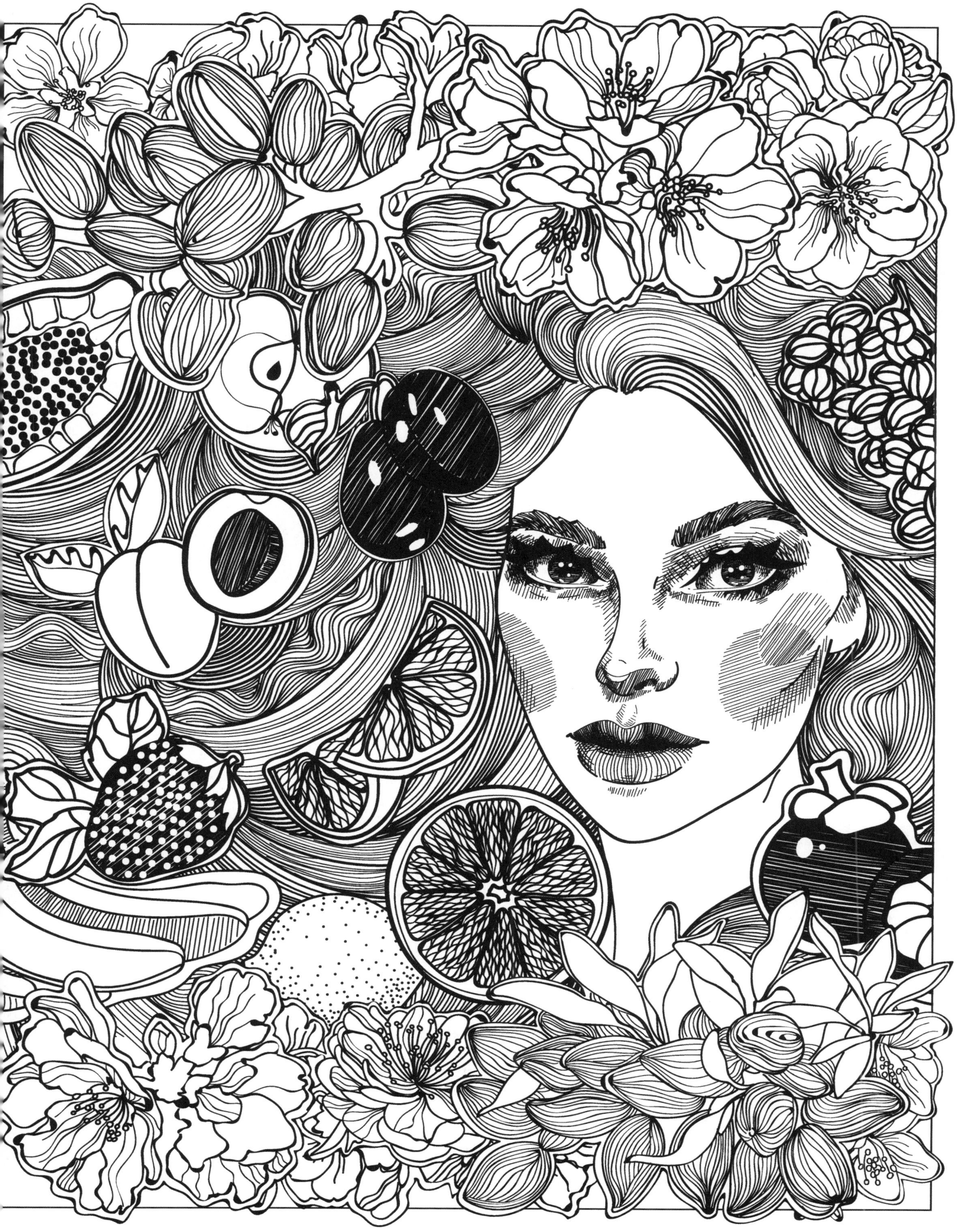

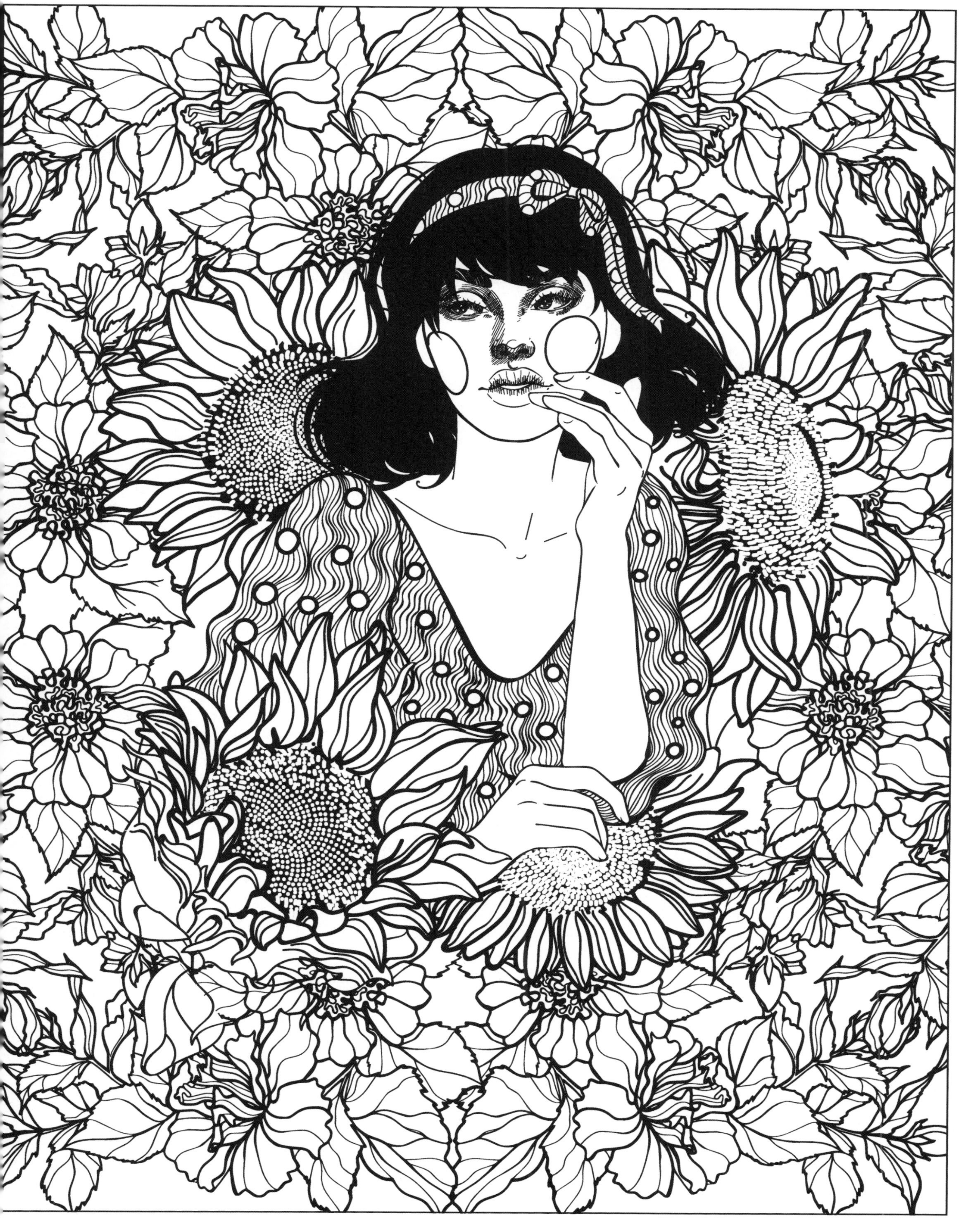

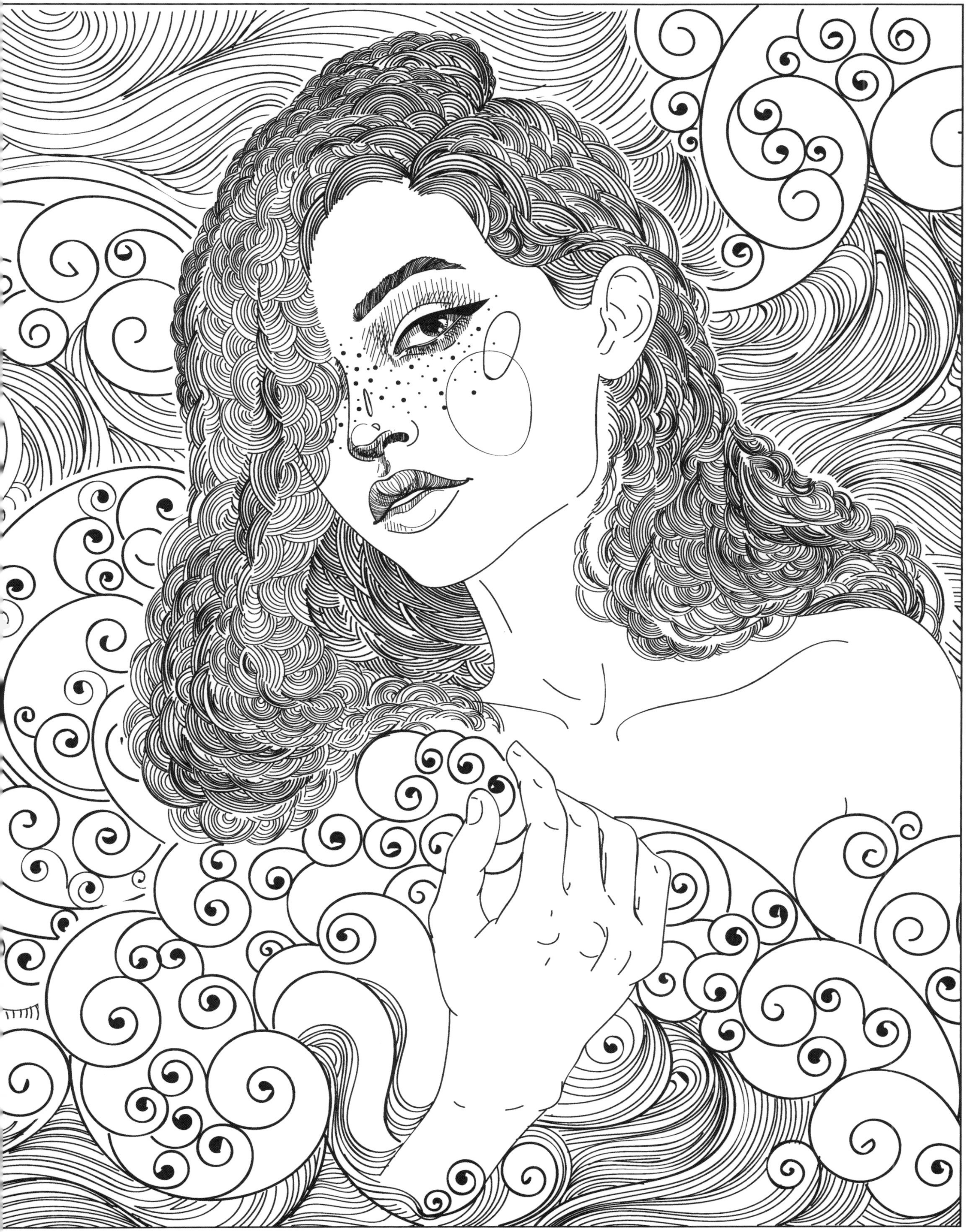

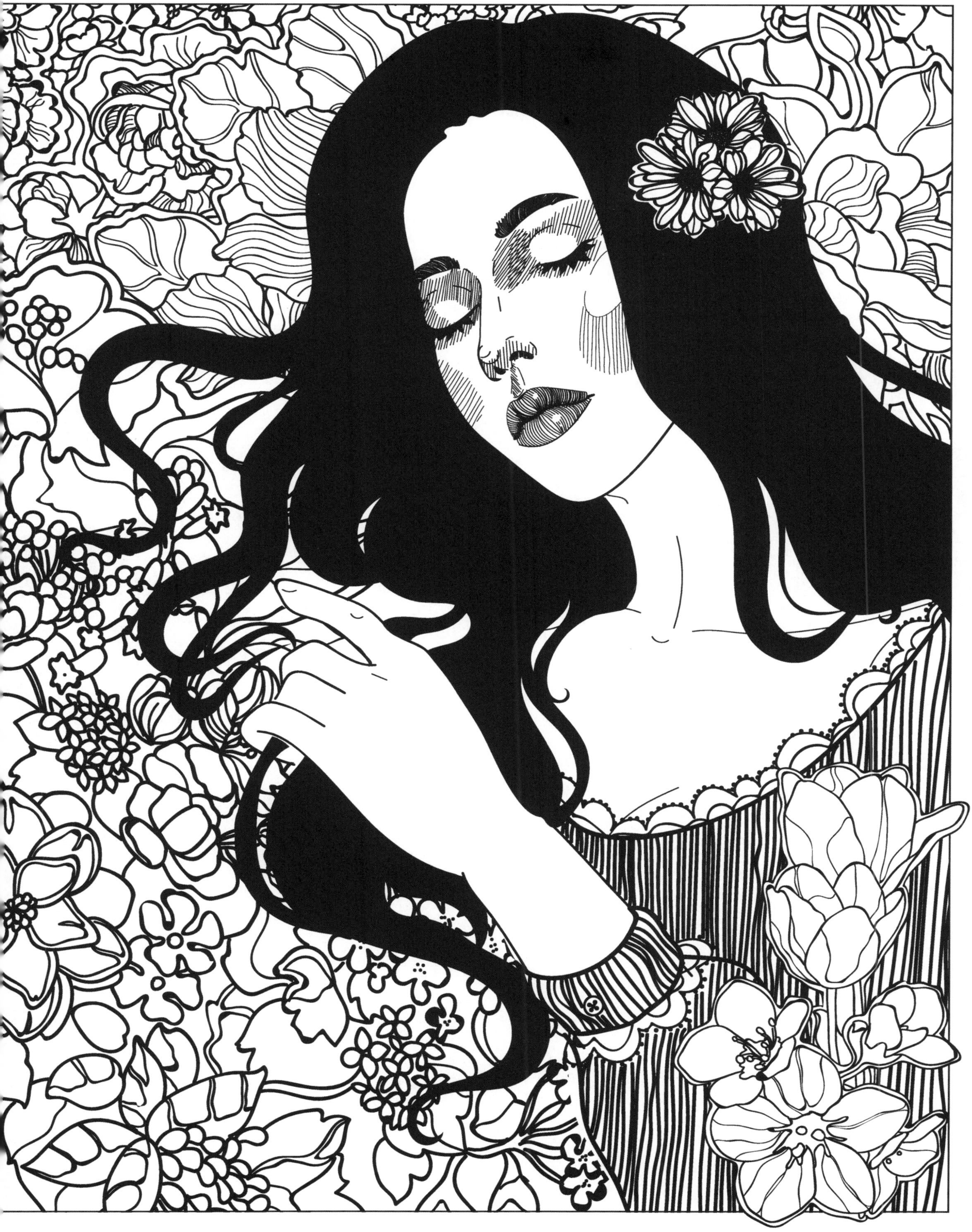

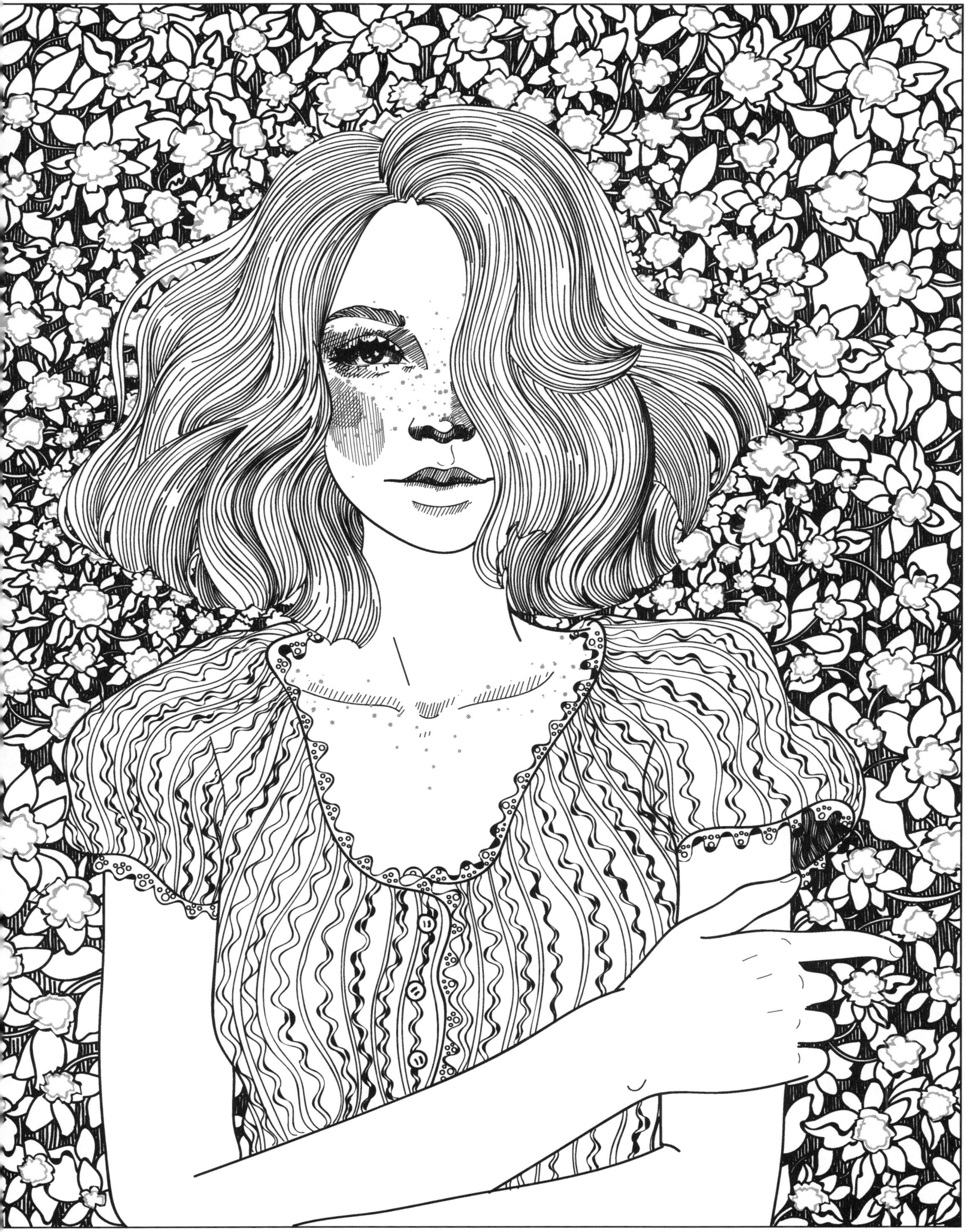

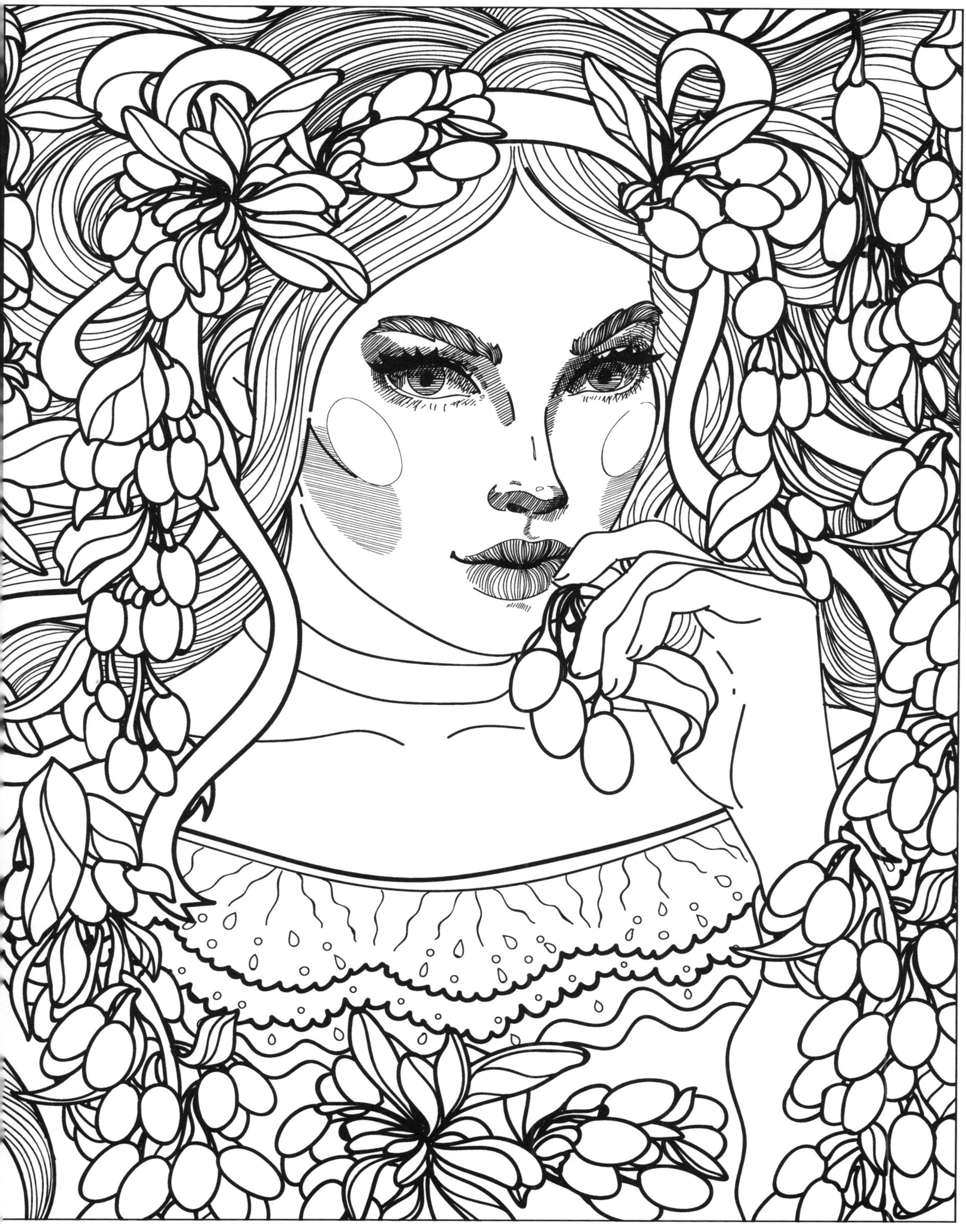

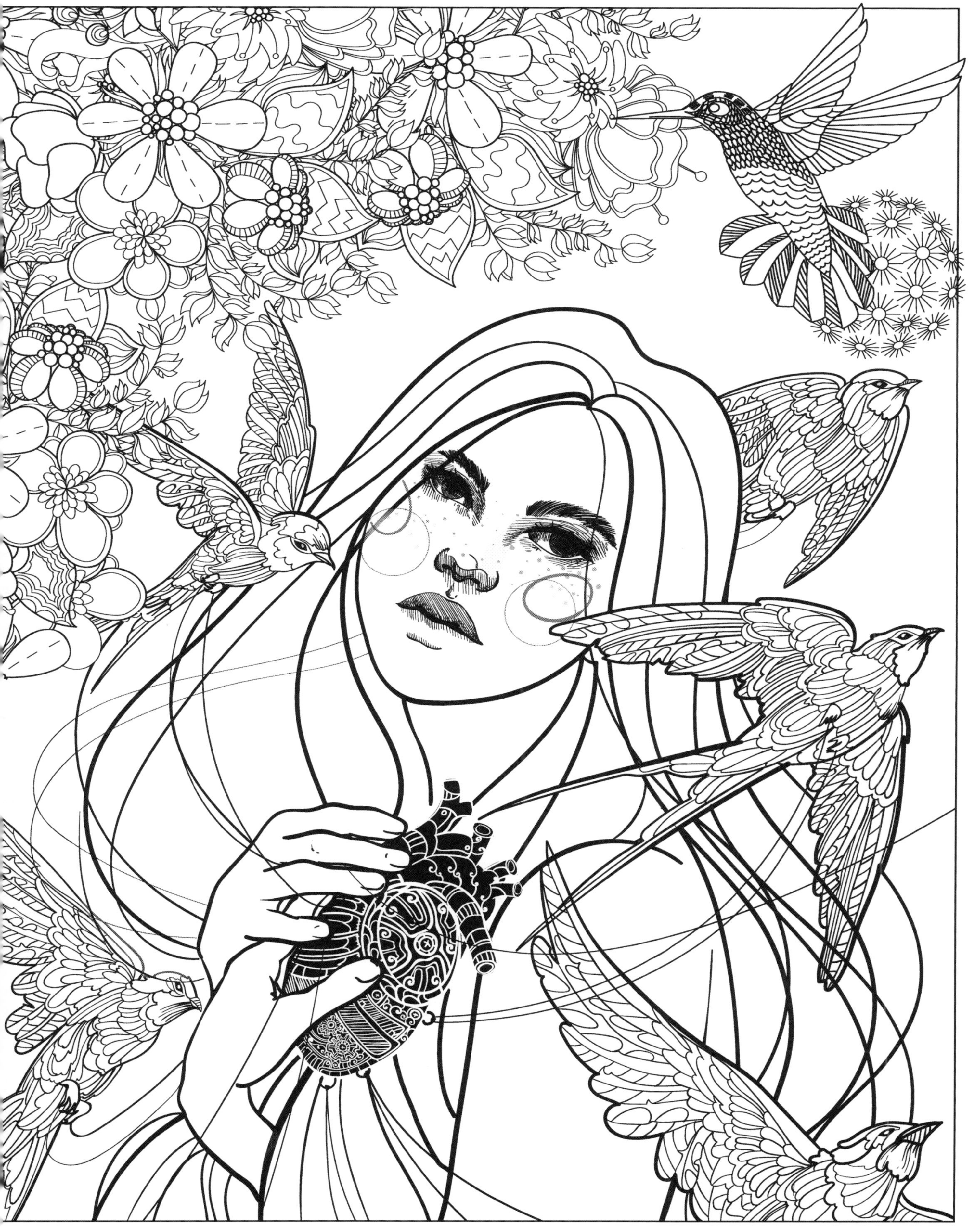

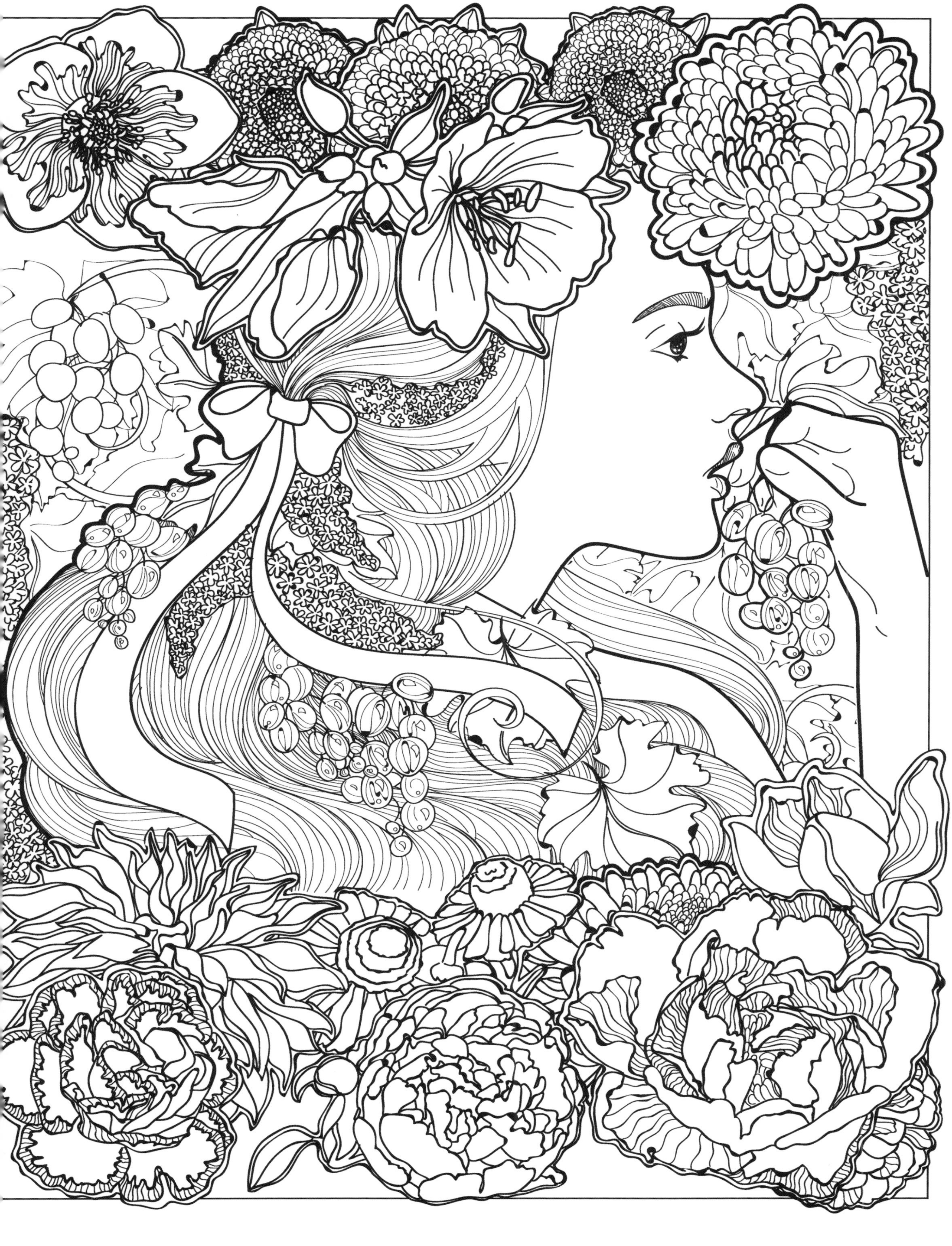

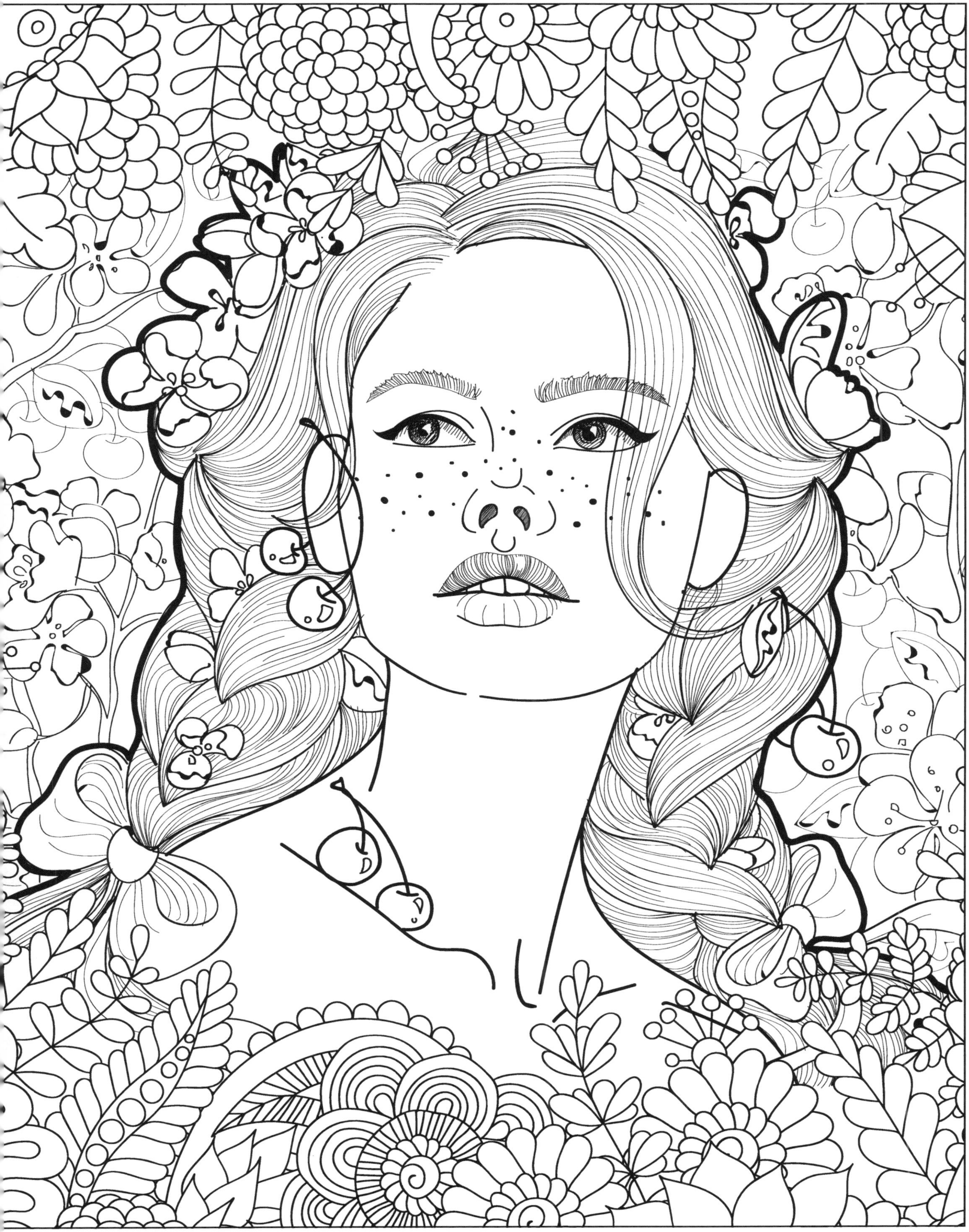

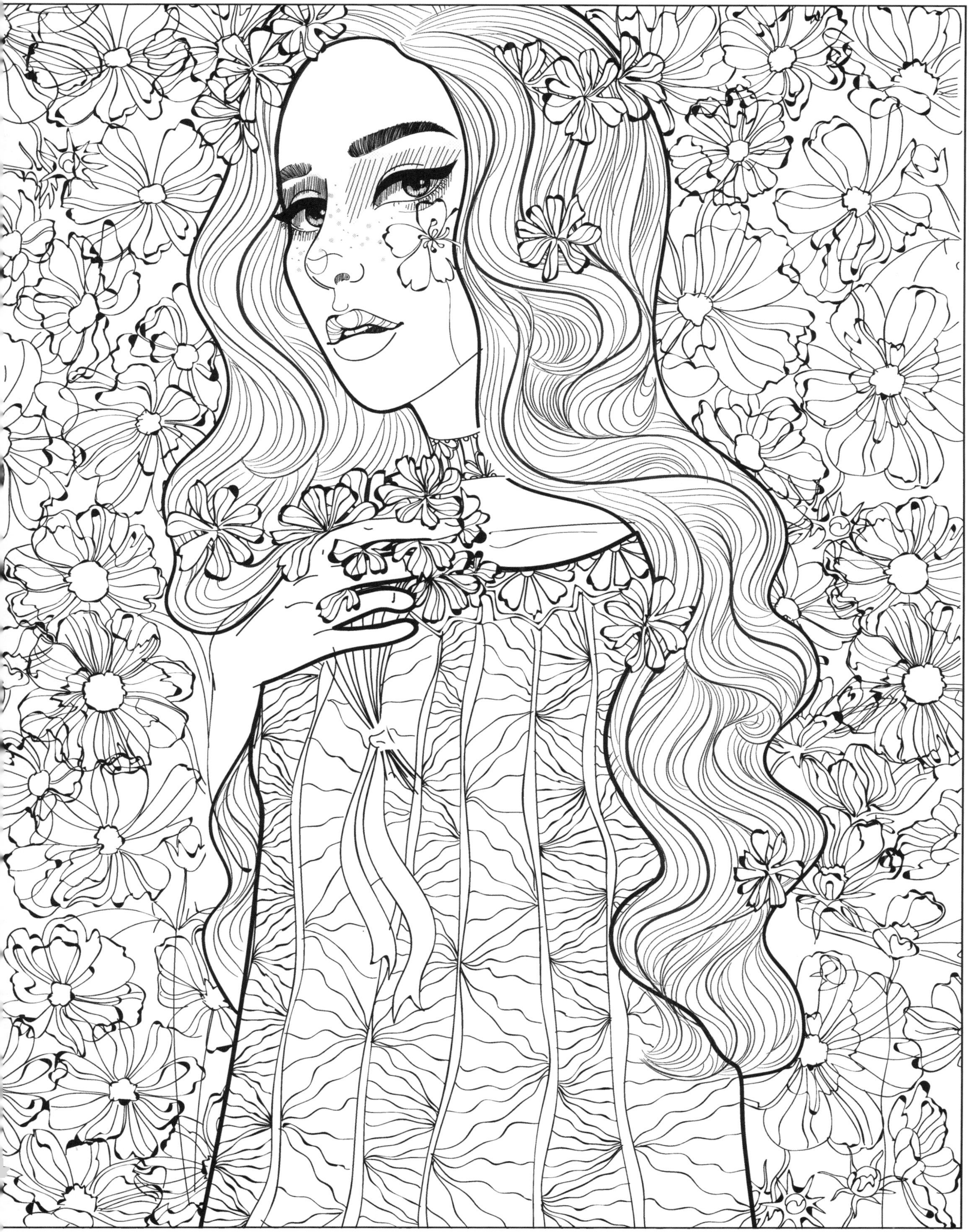

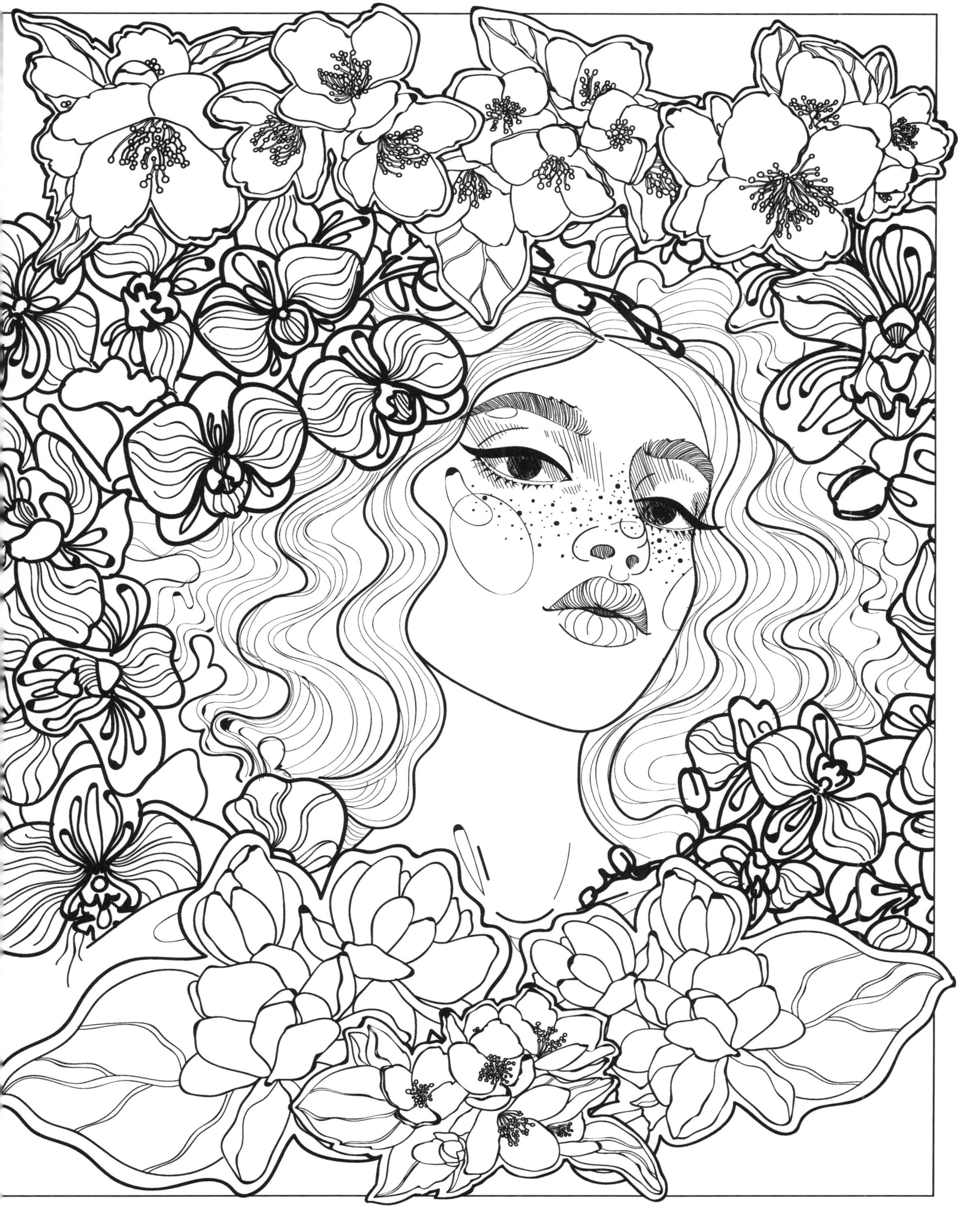

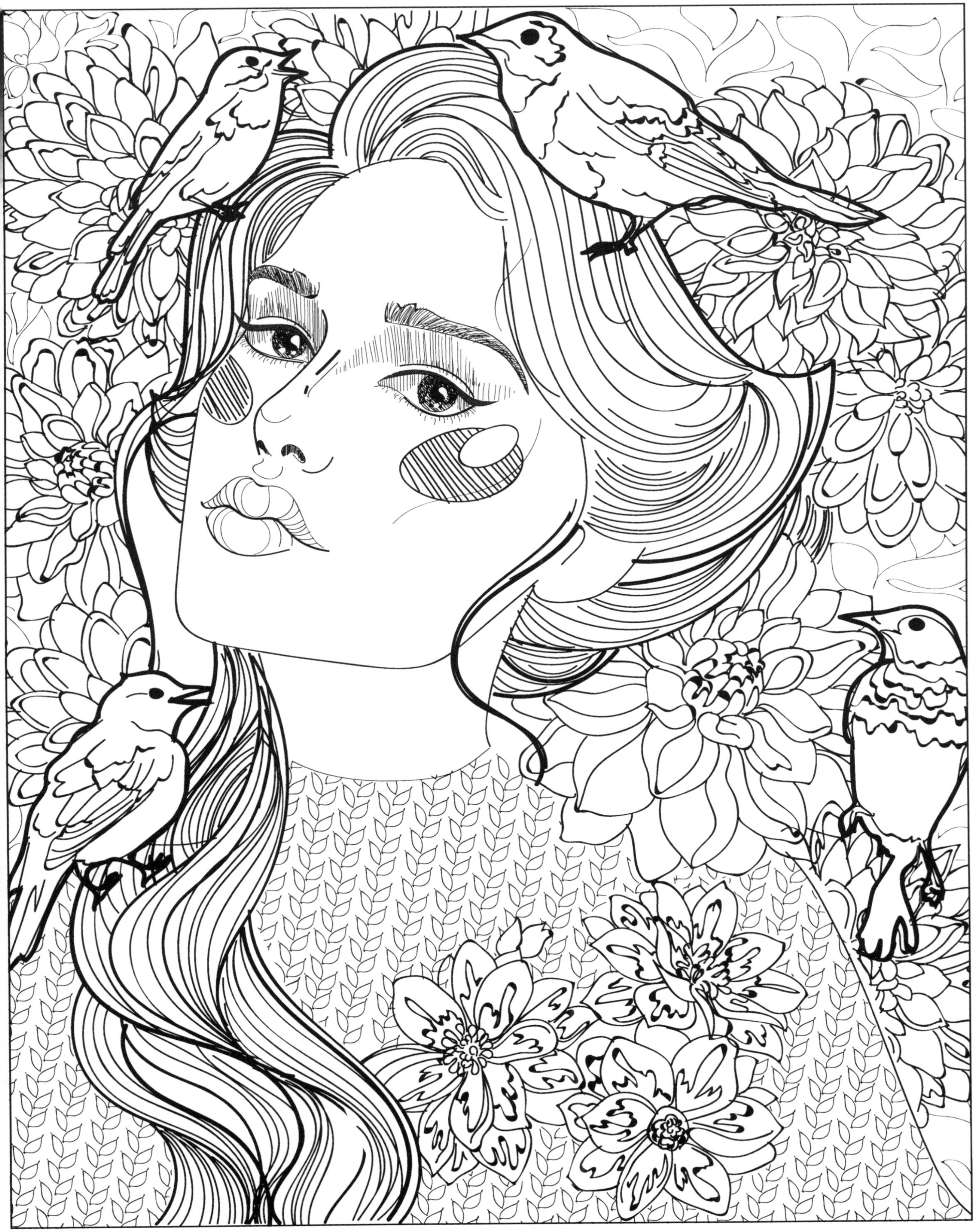

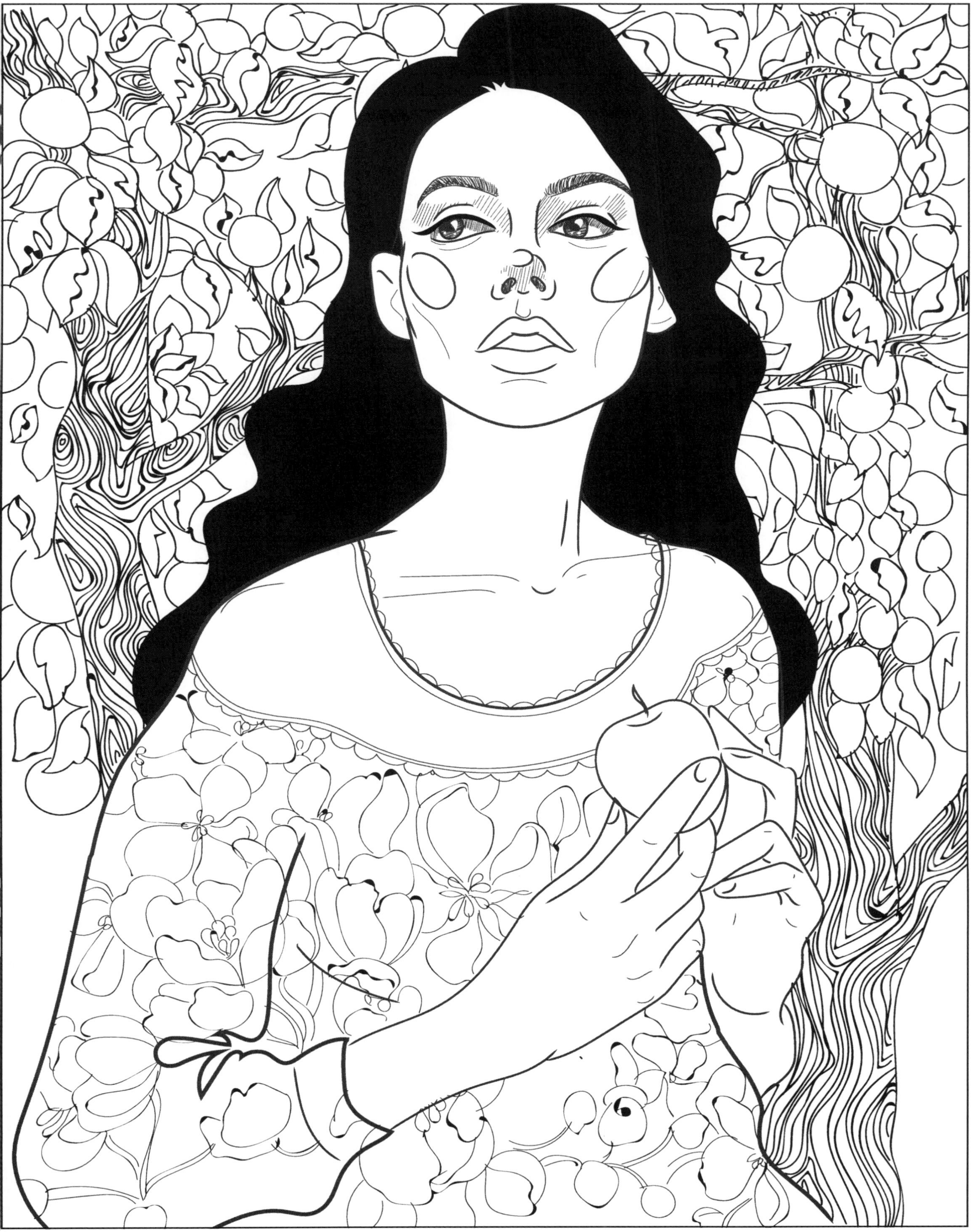

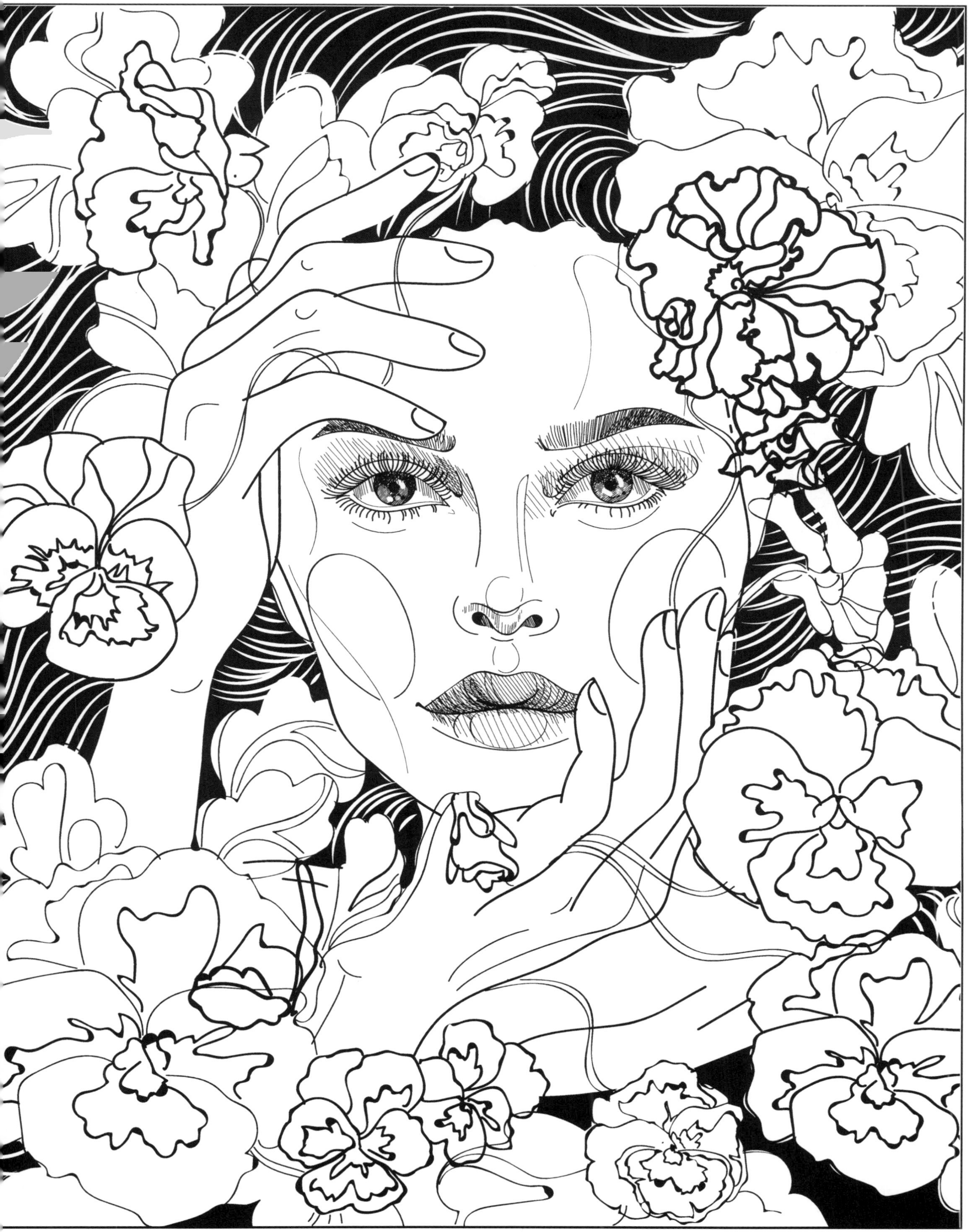

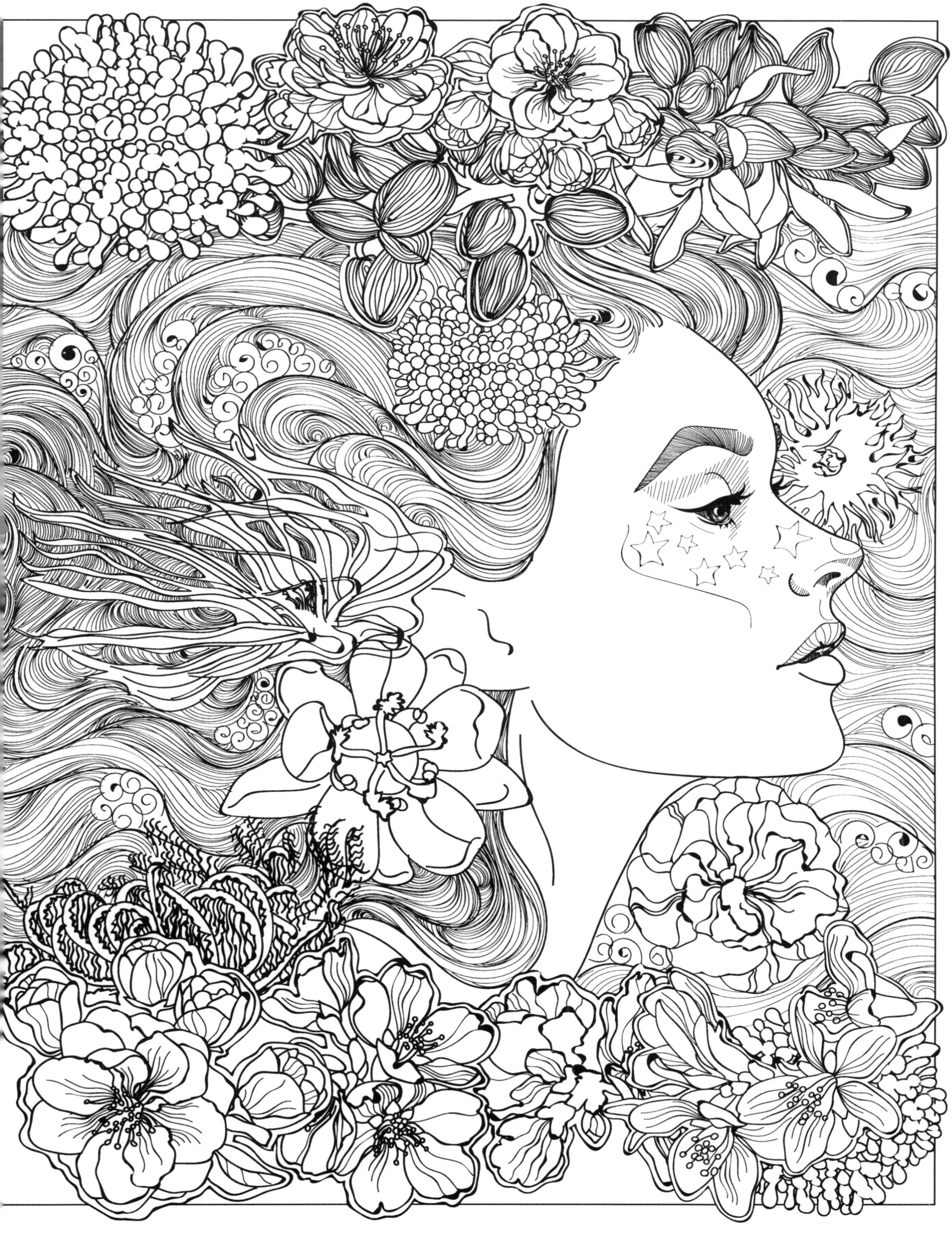

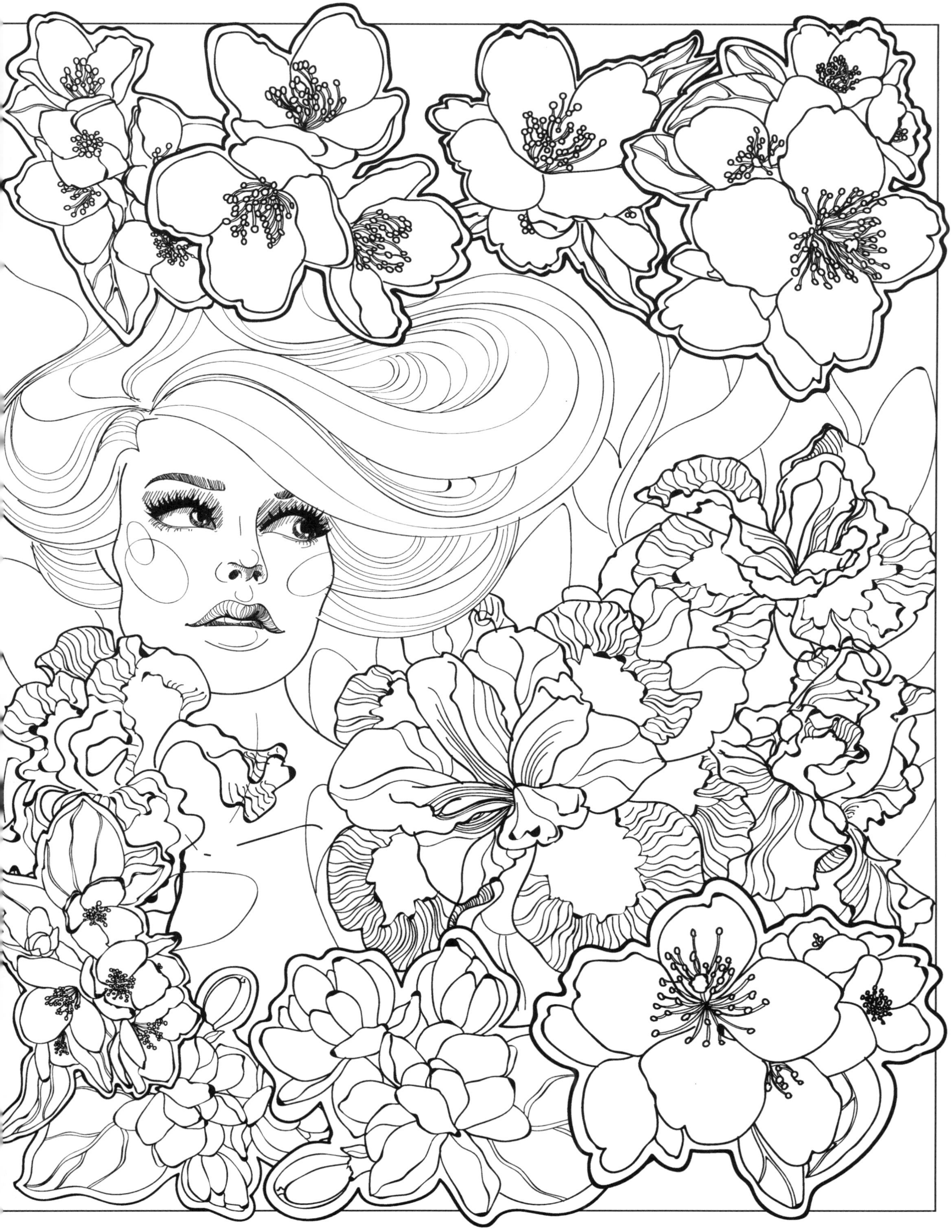

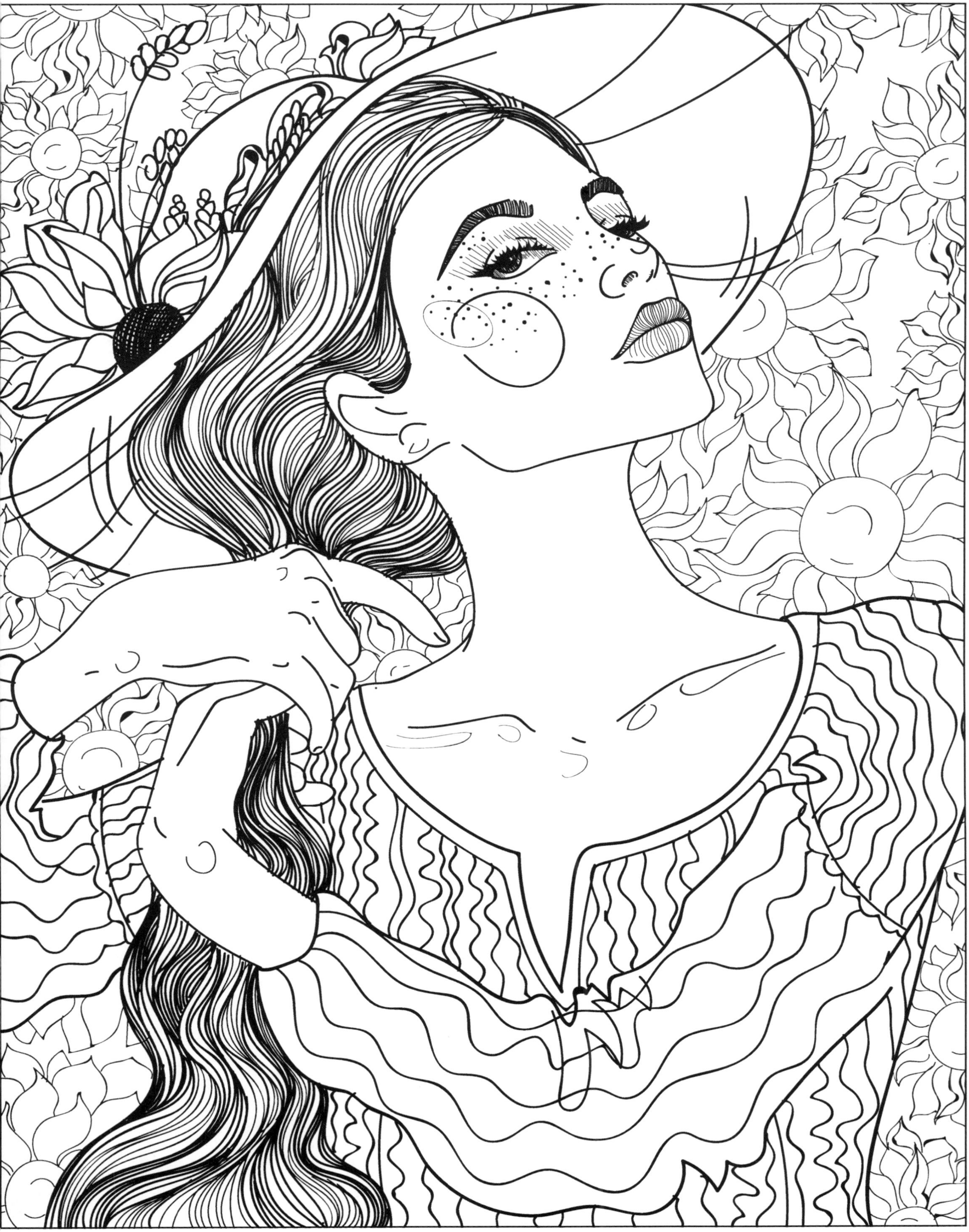

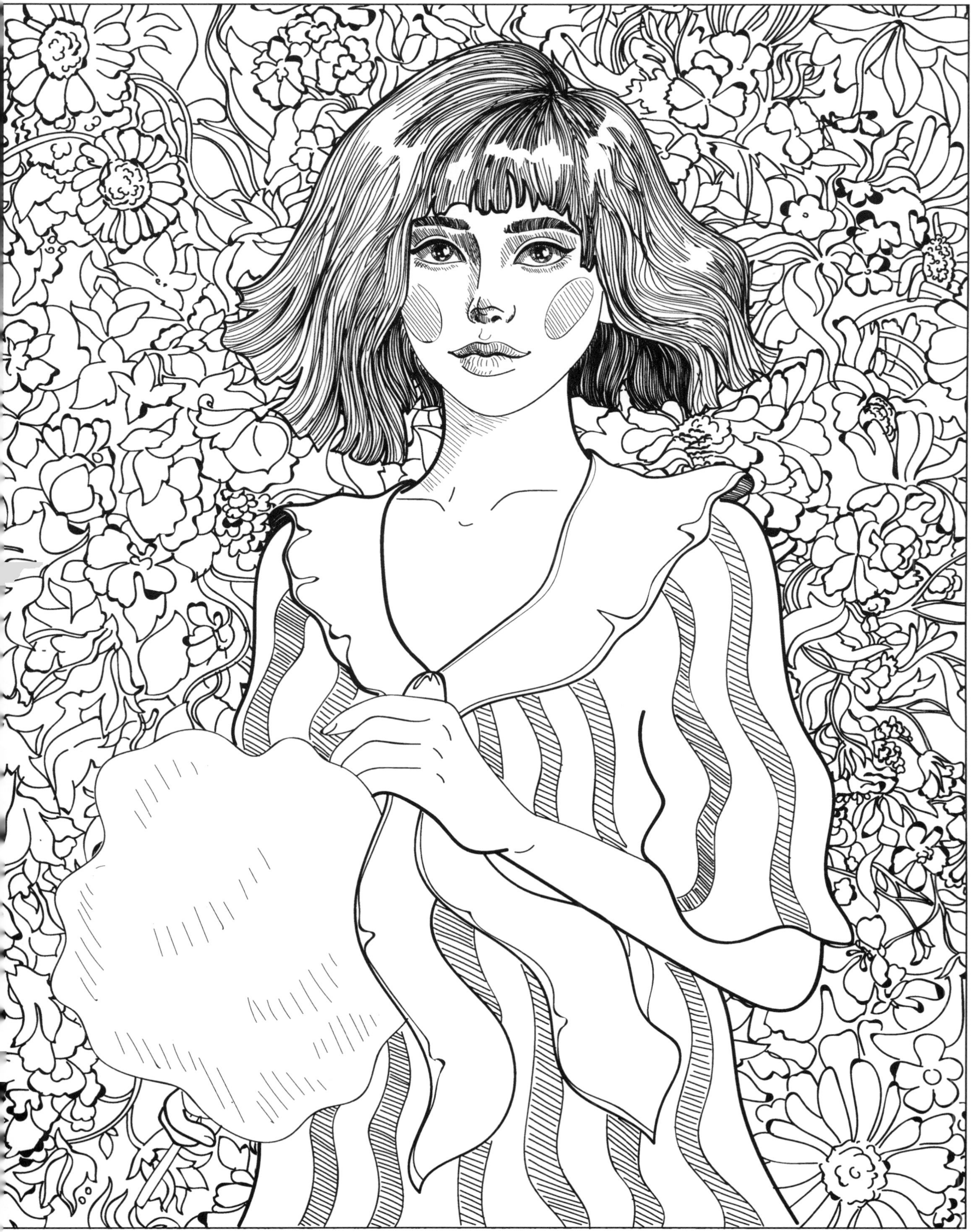

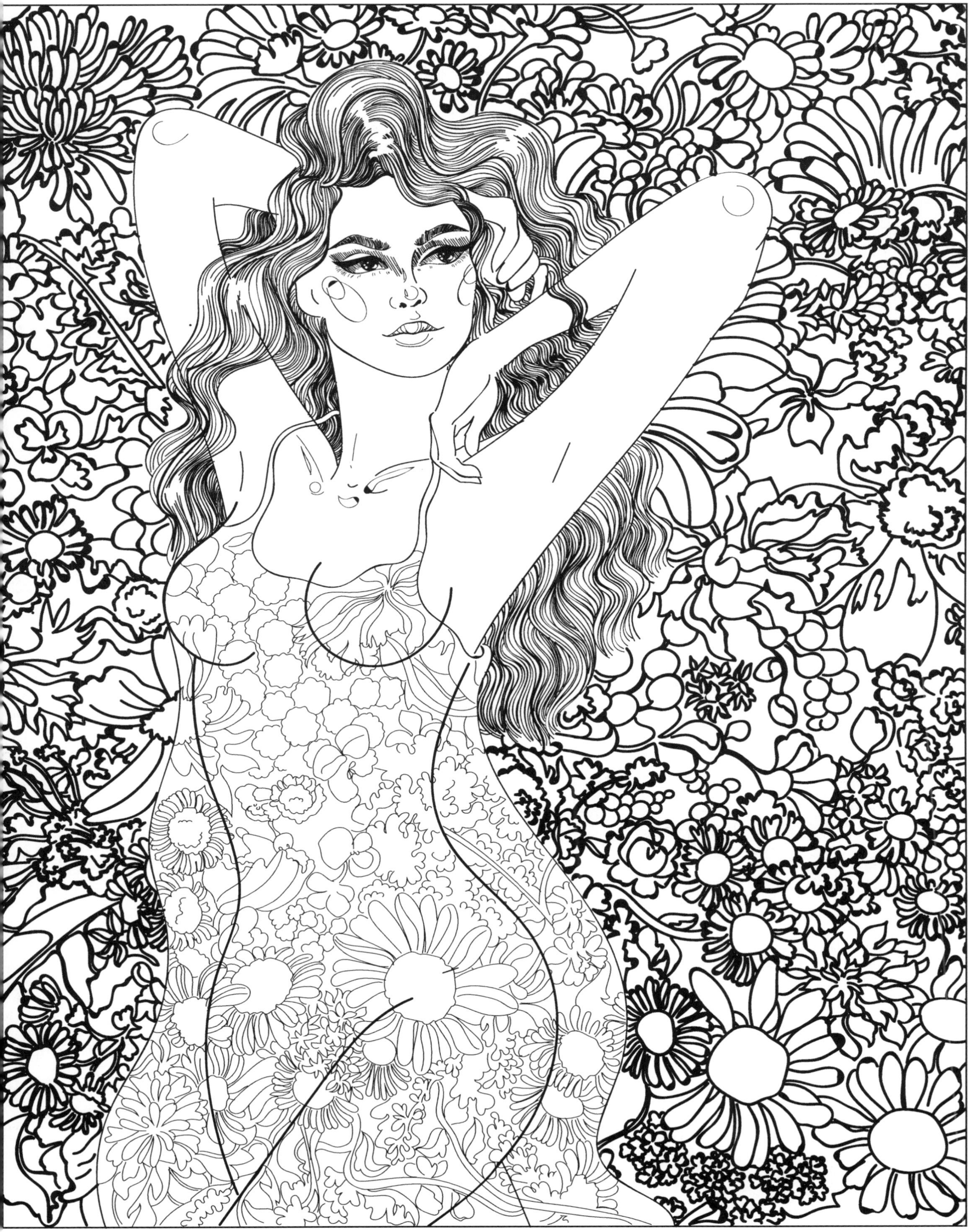

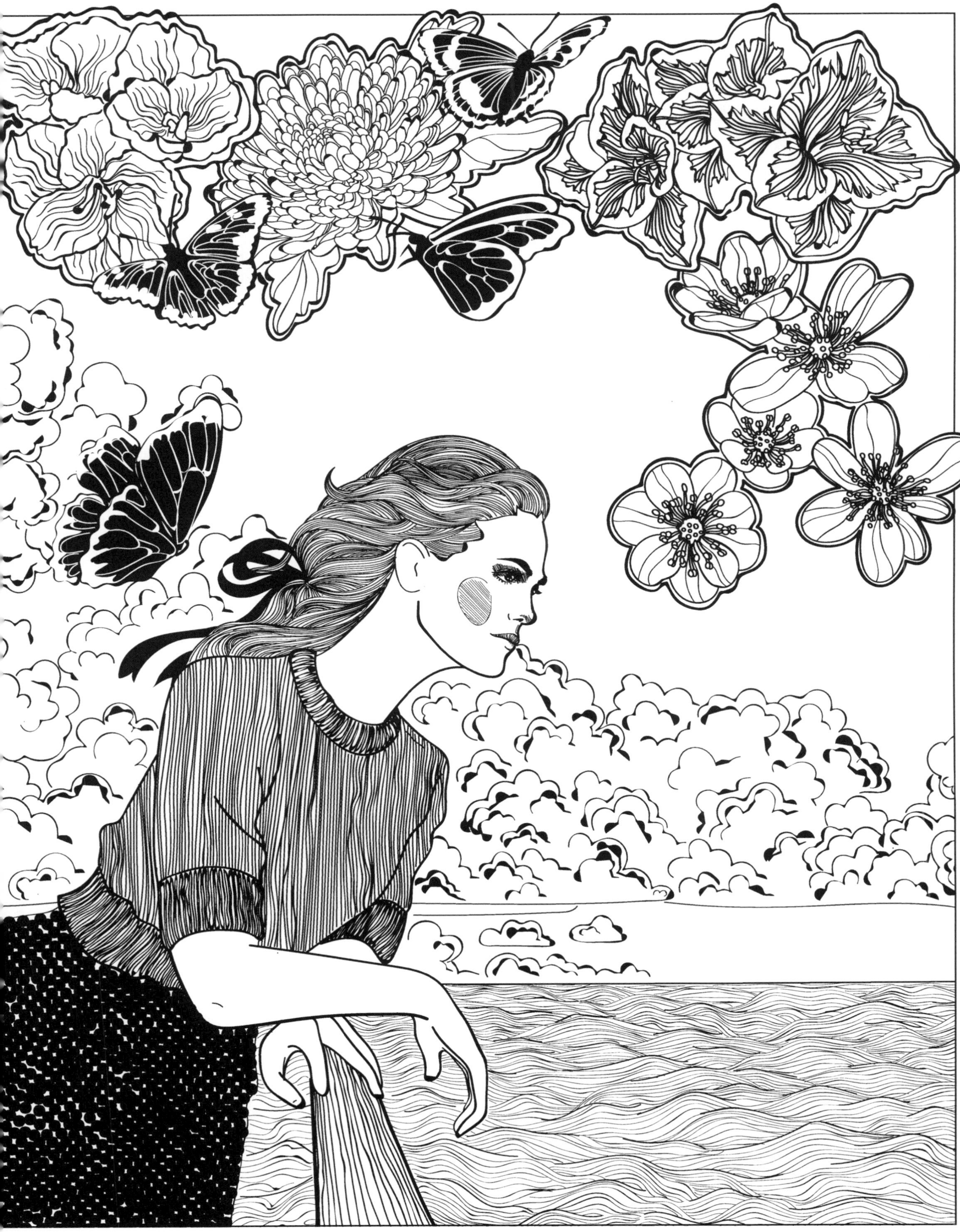

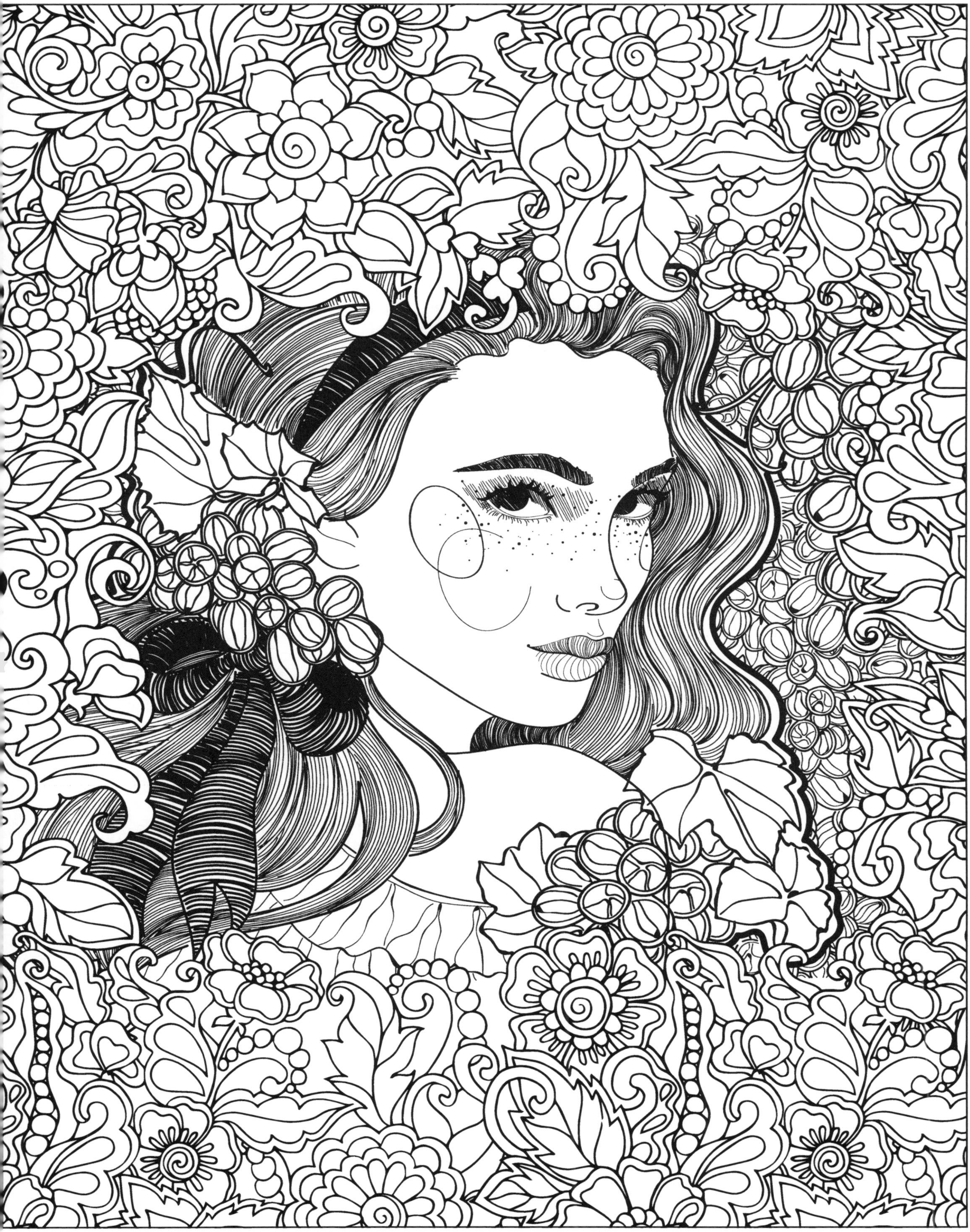

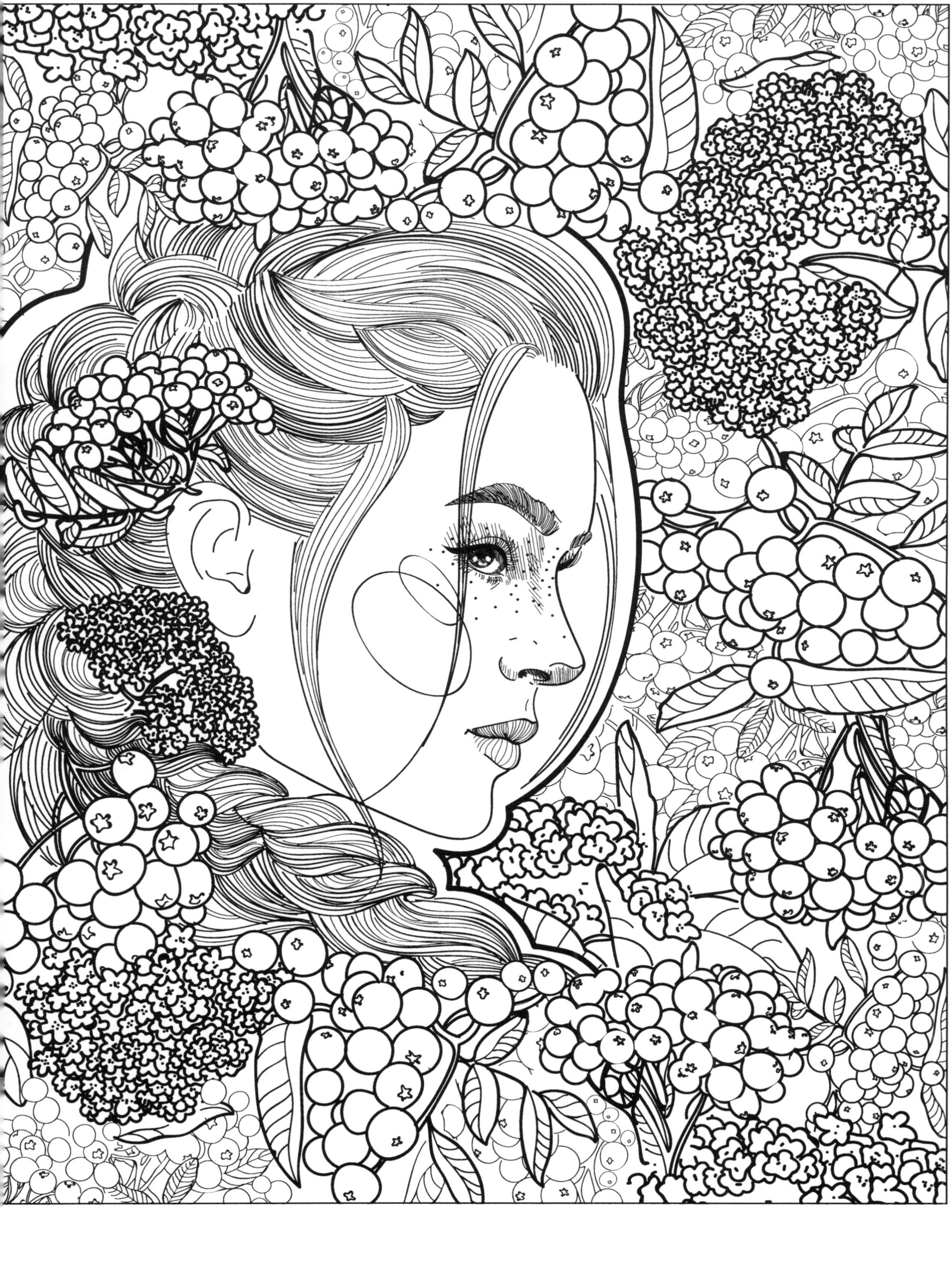

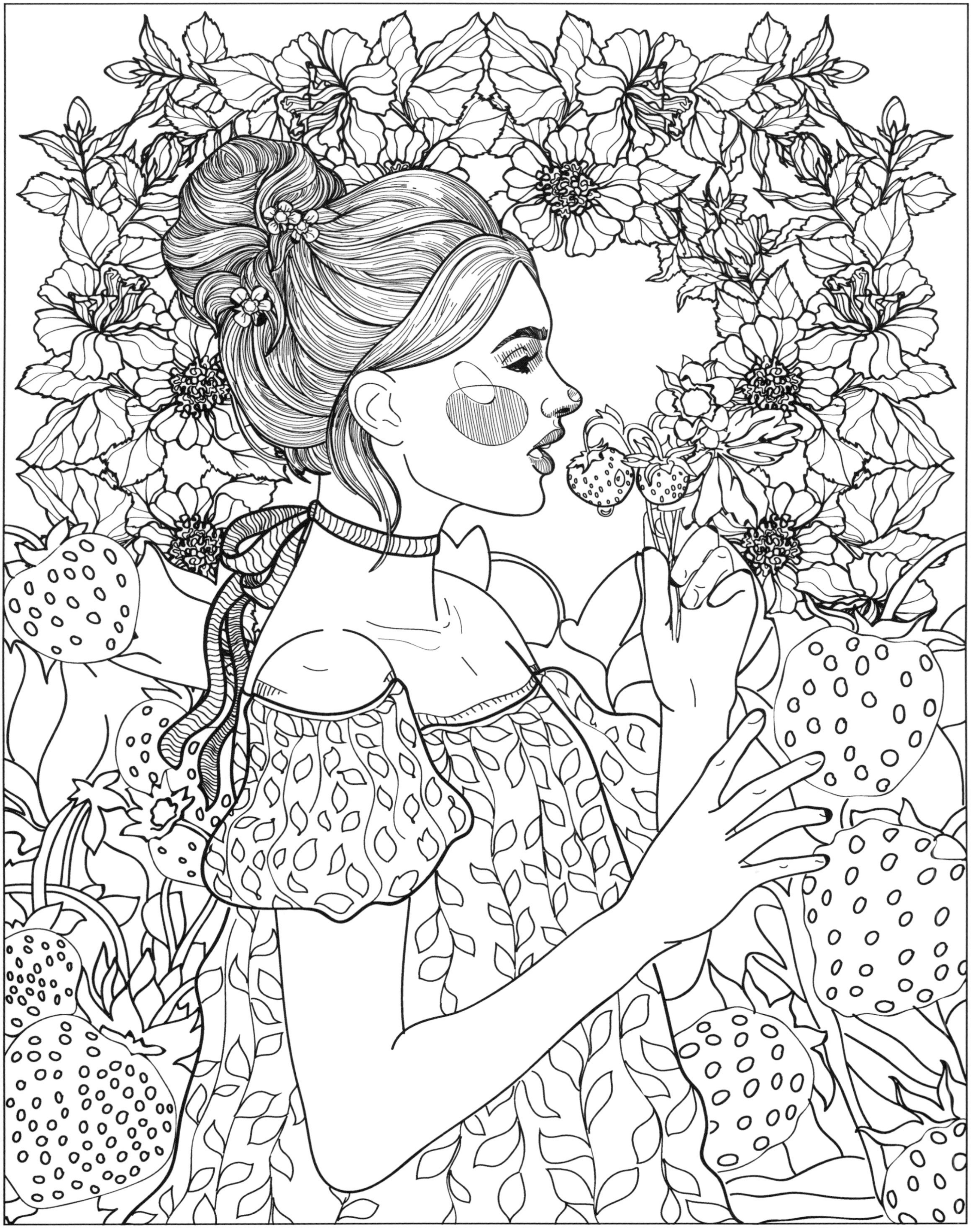

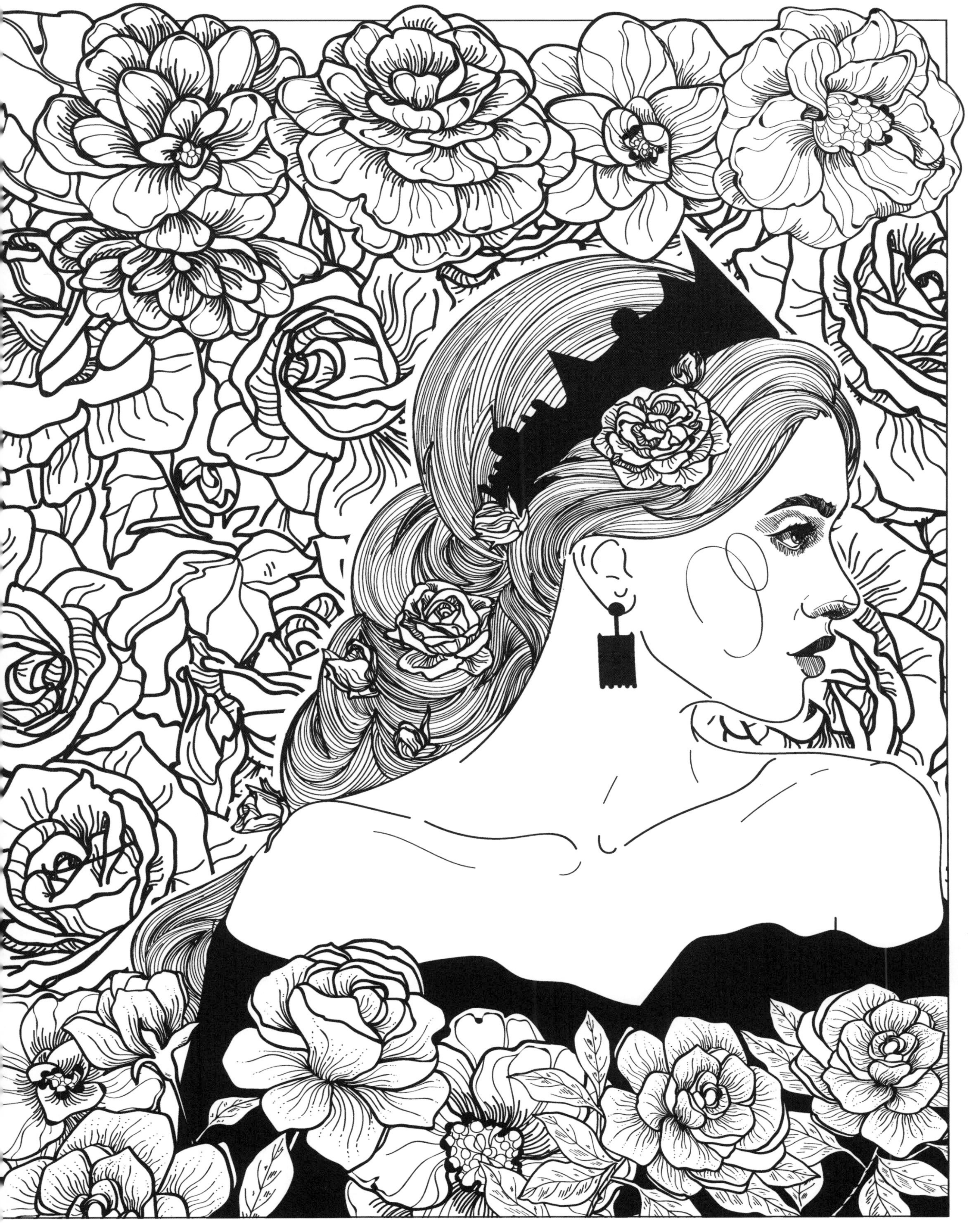

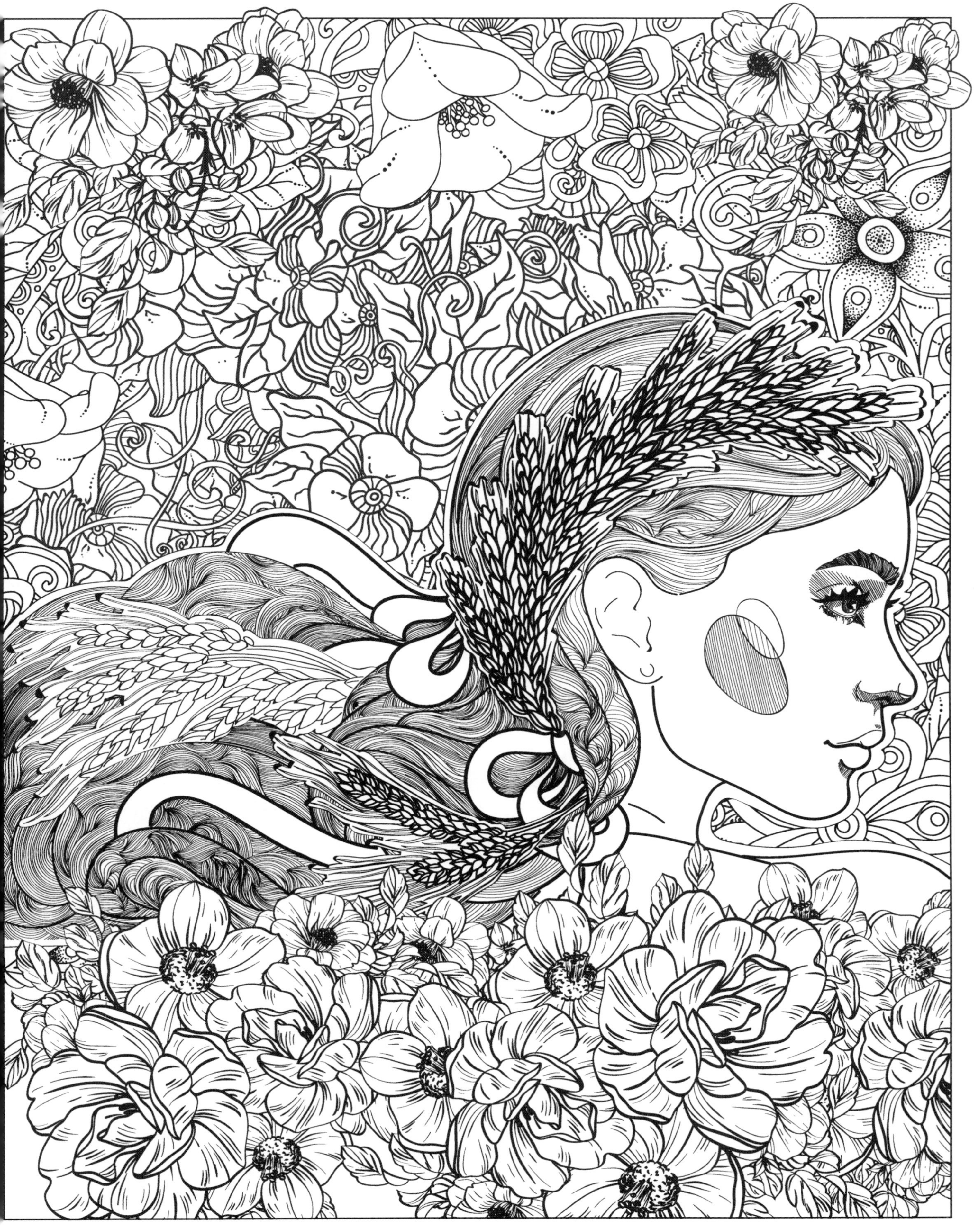

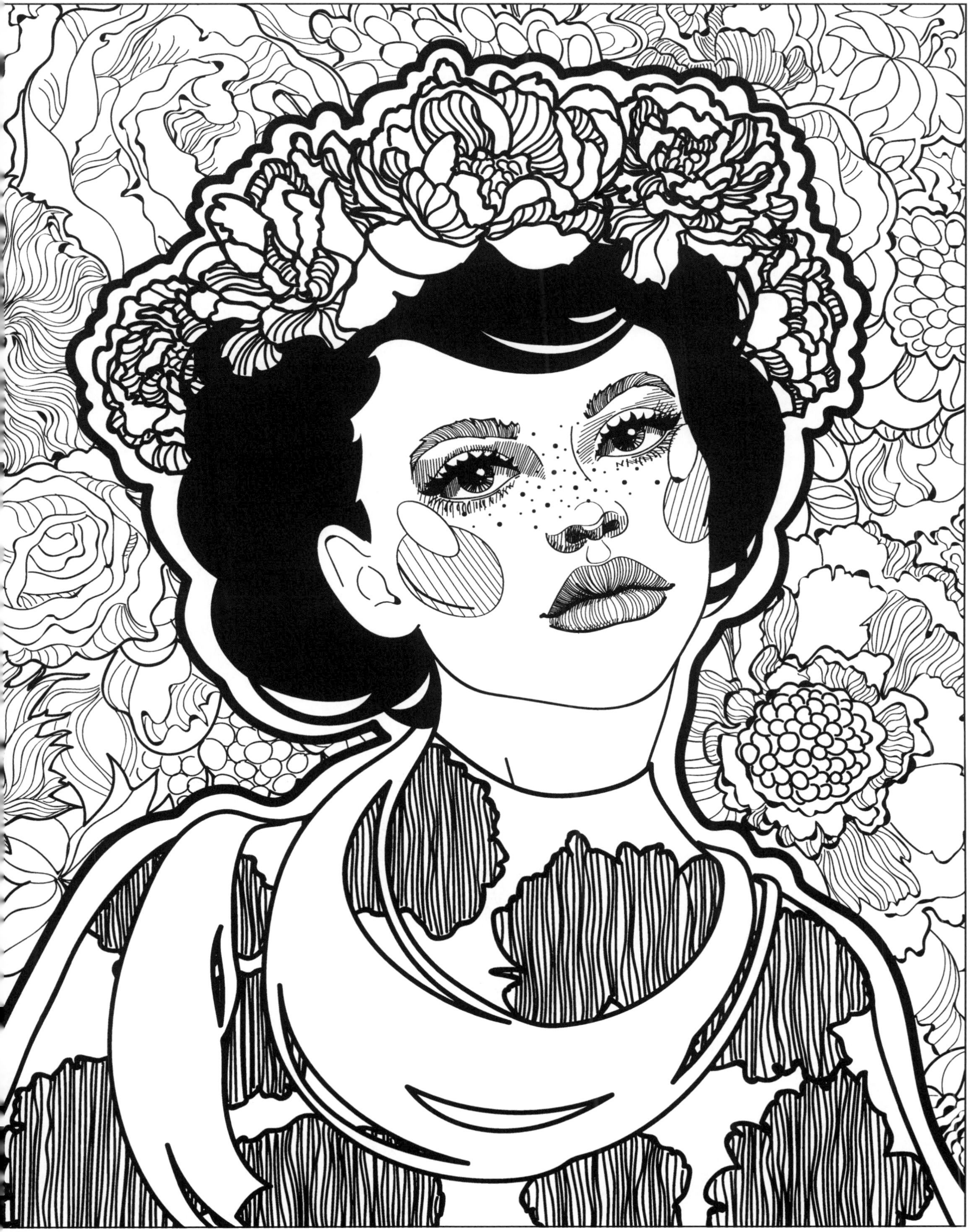

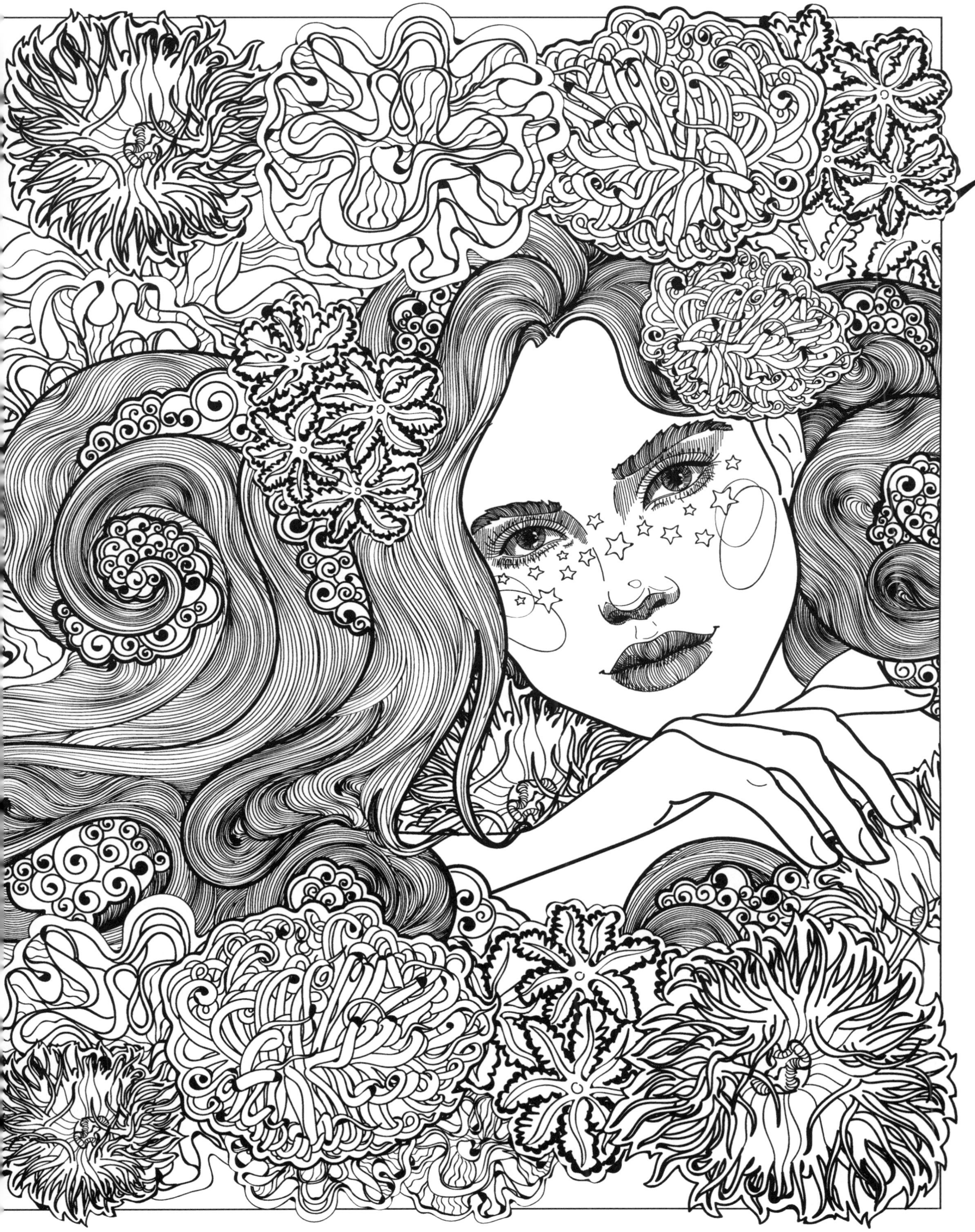

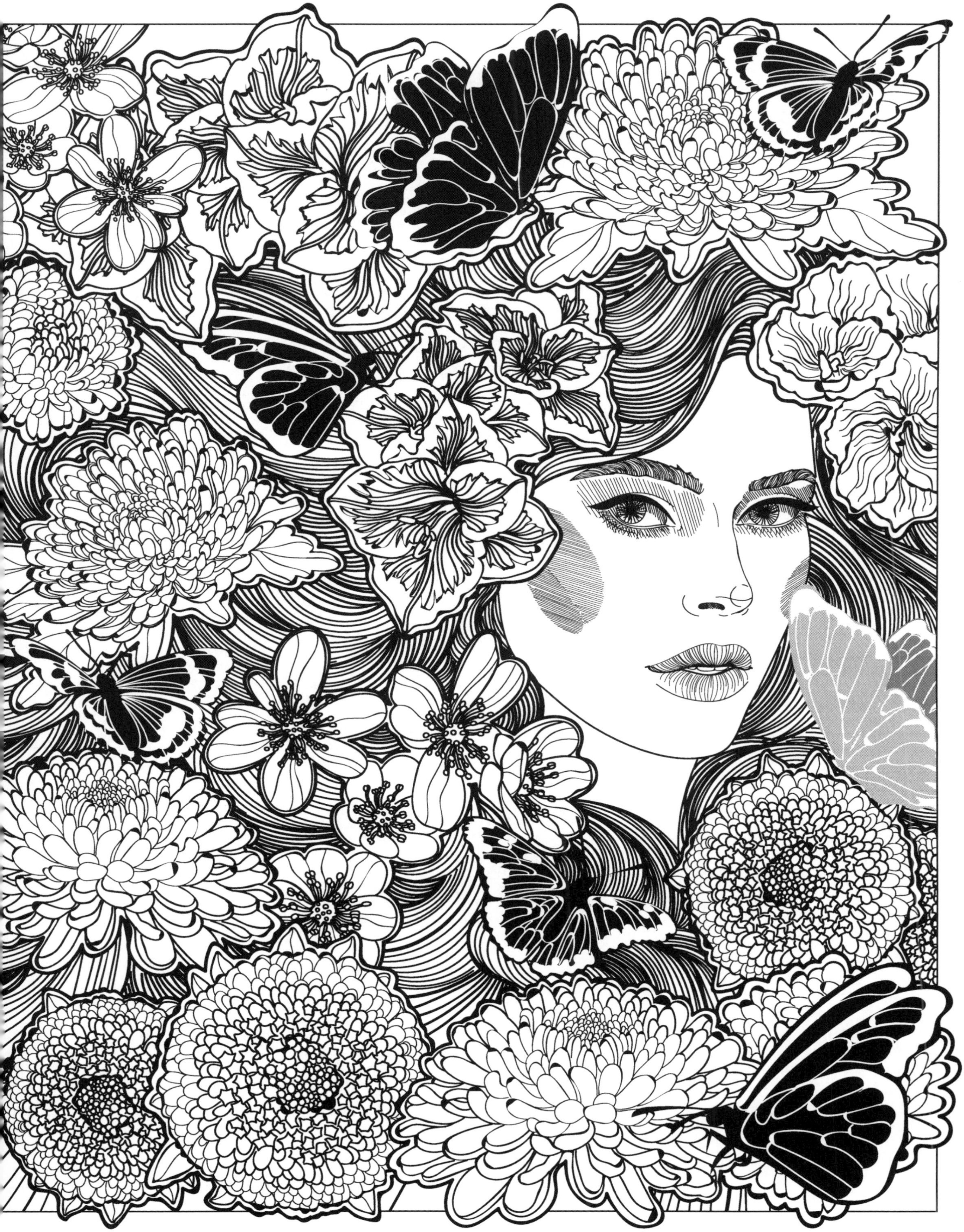

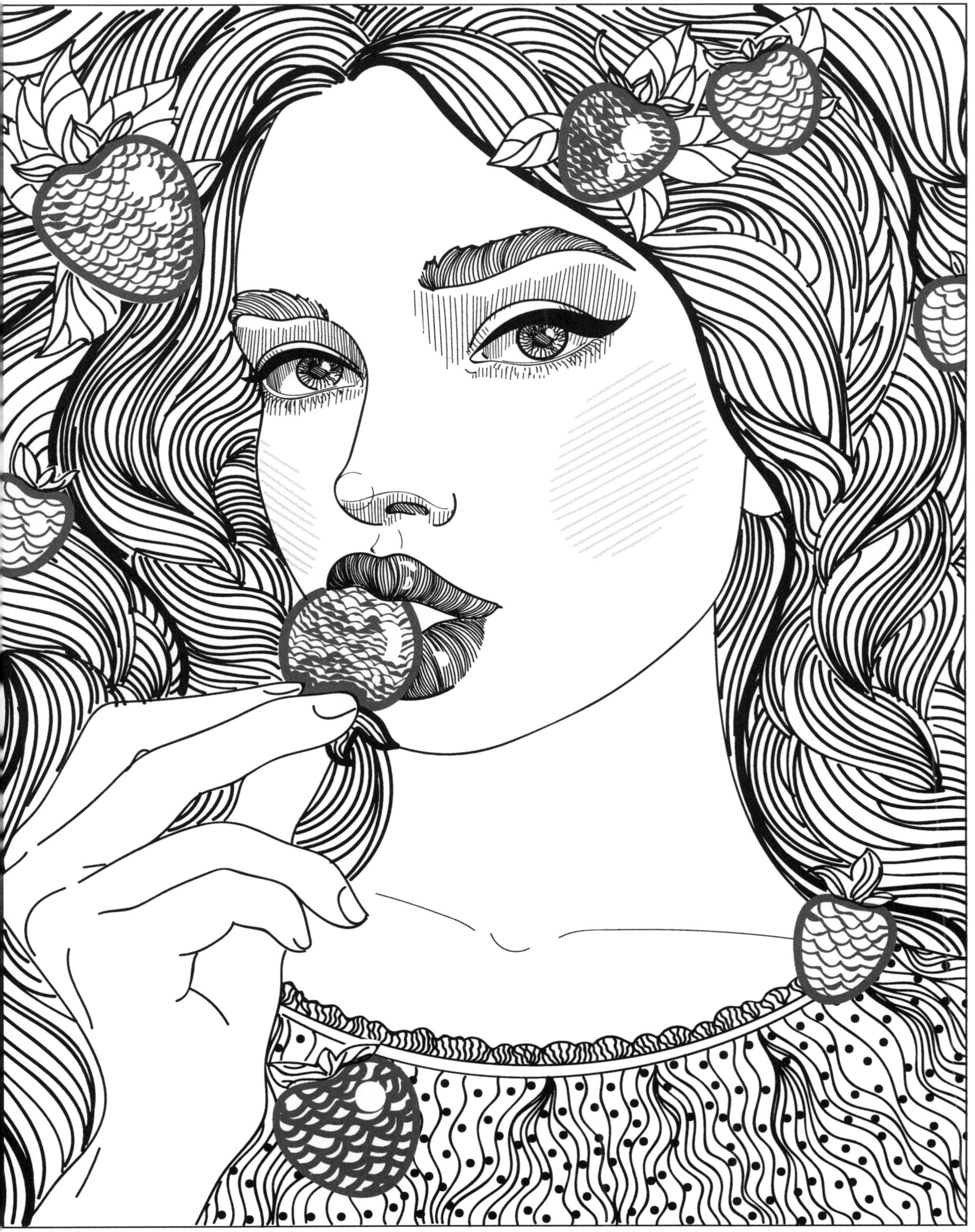

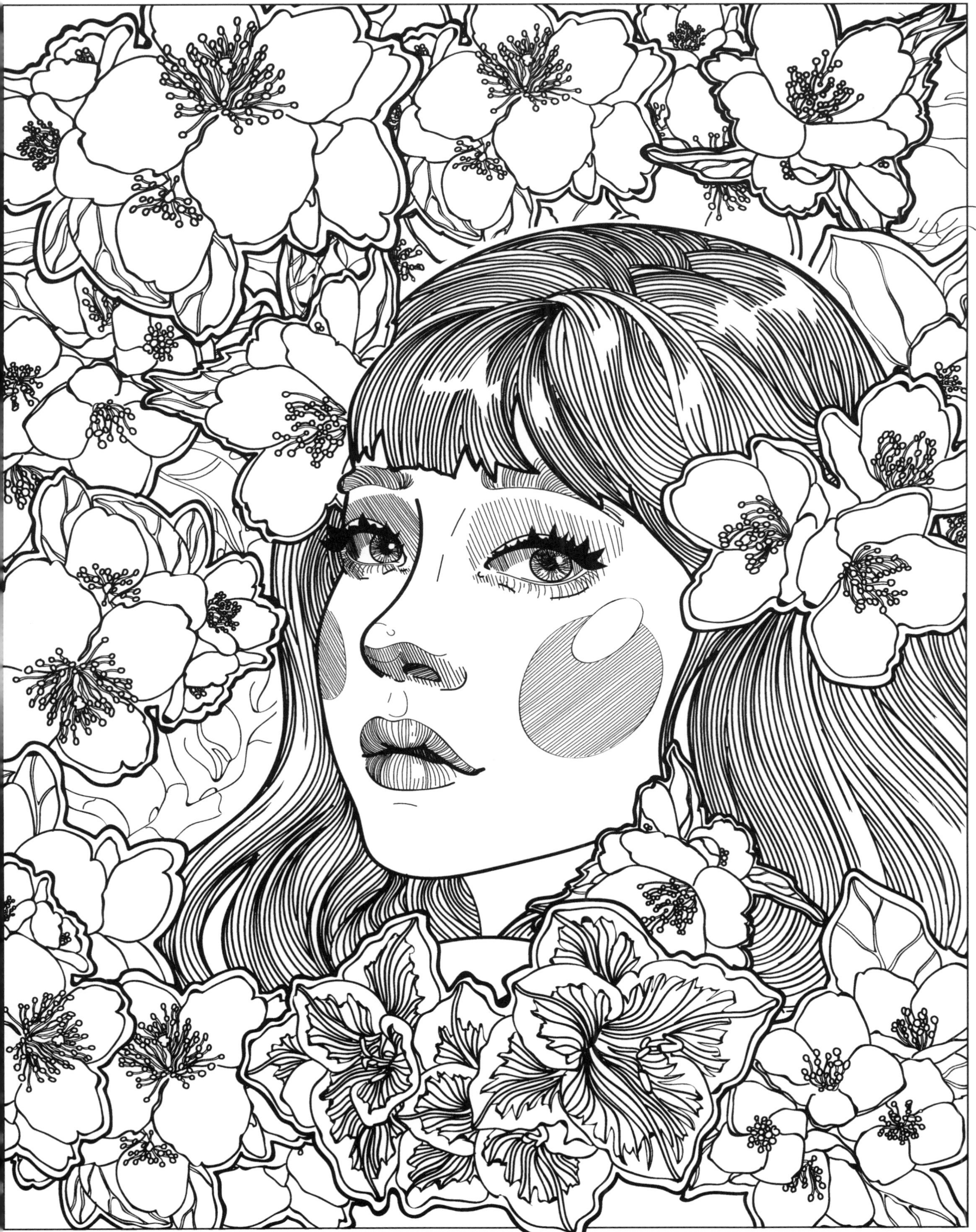

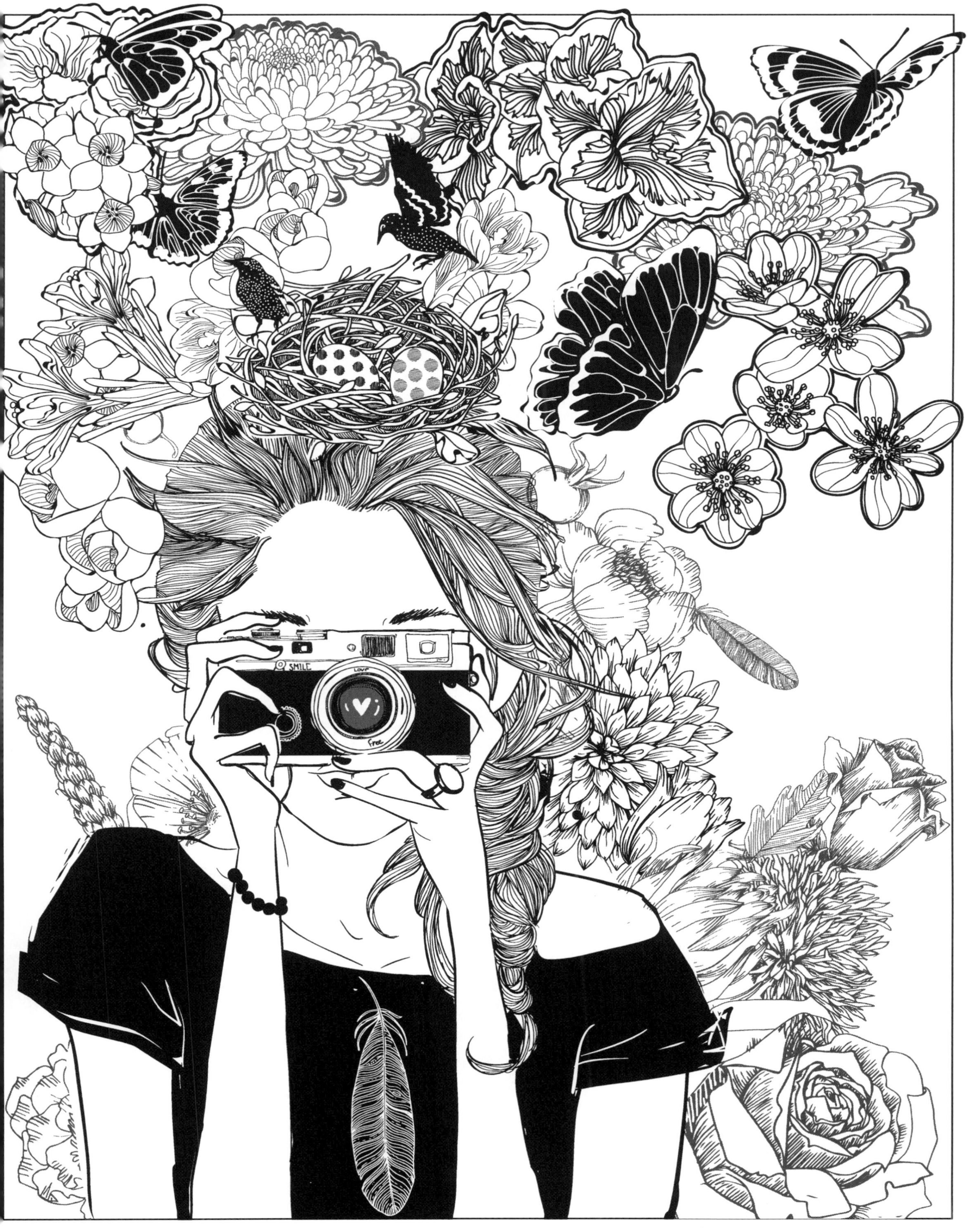
SMILE
Love
free

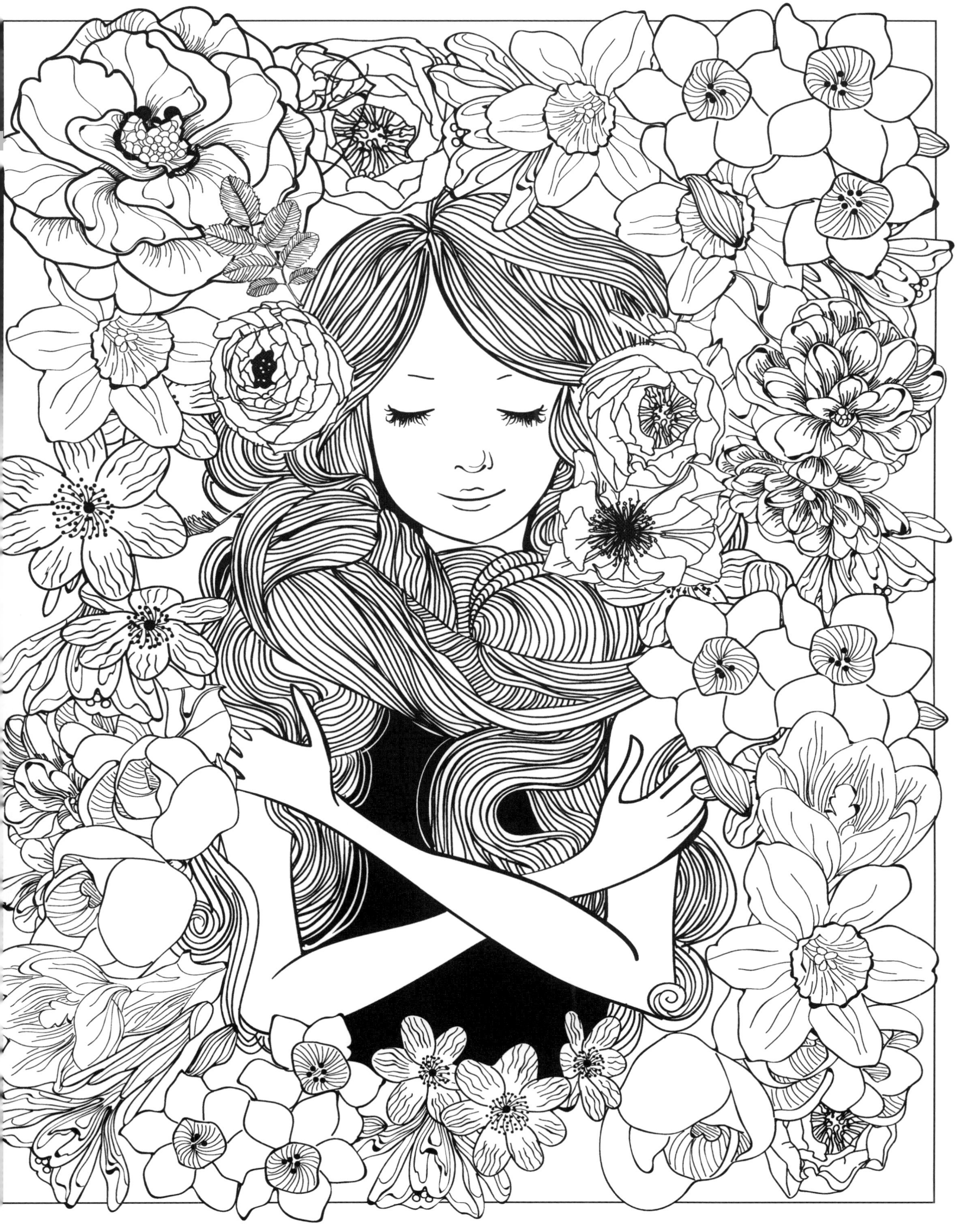

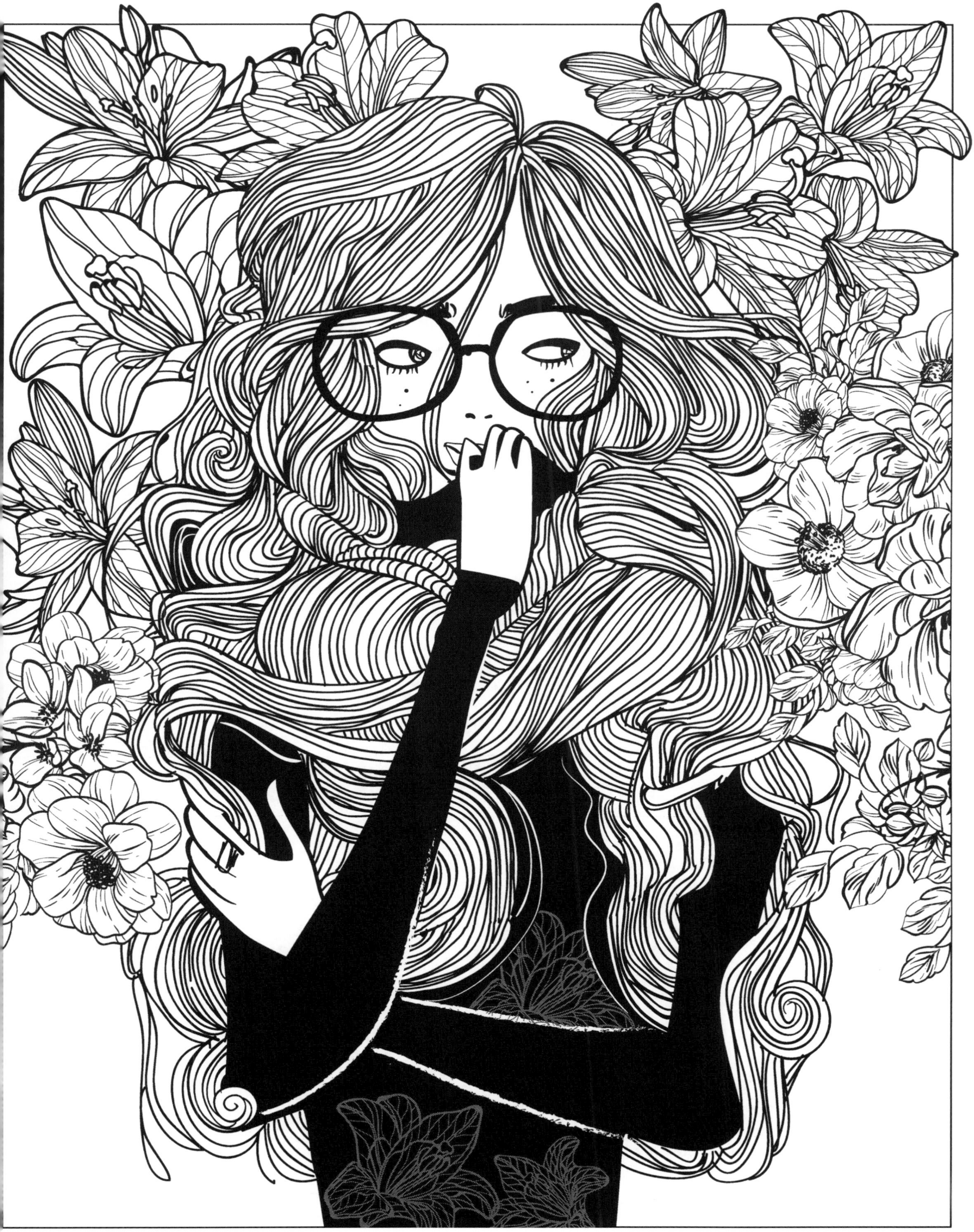

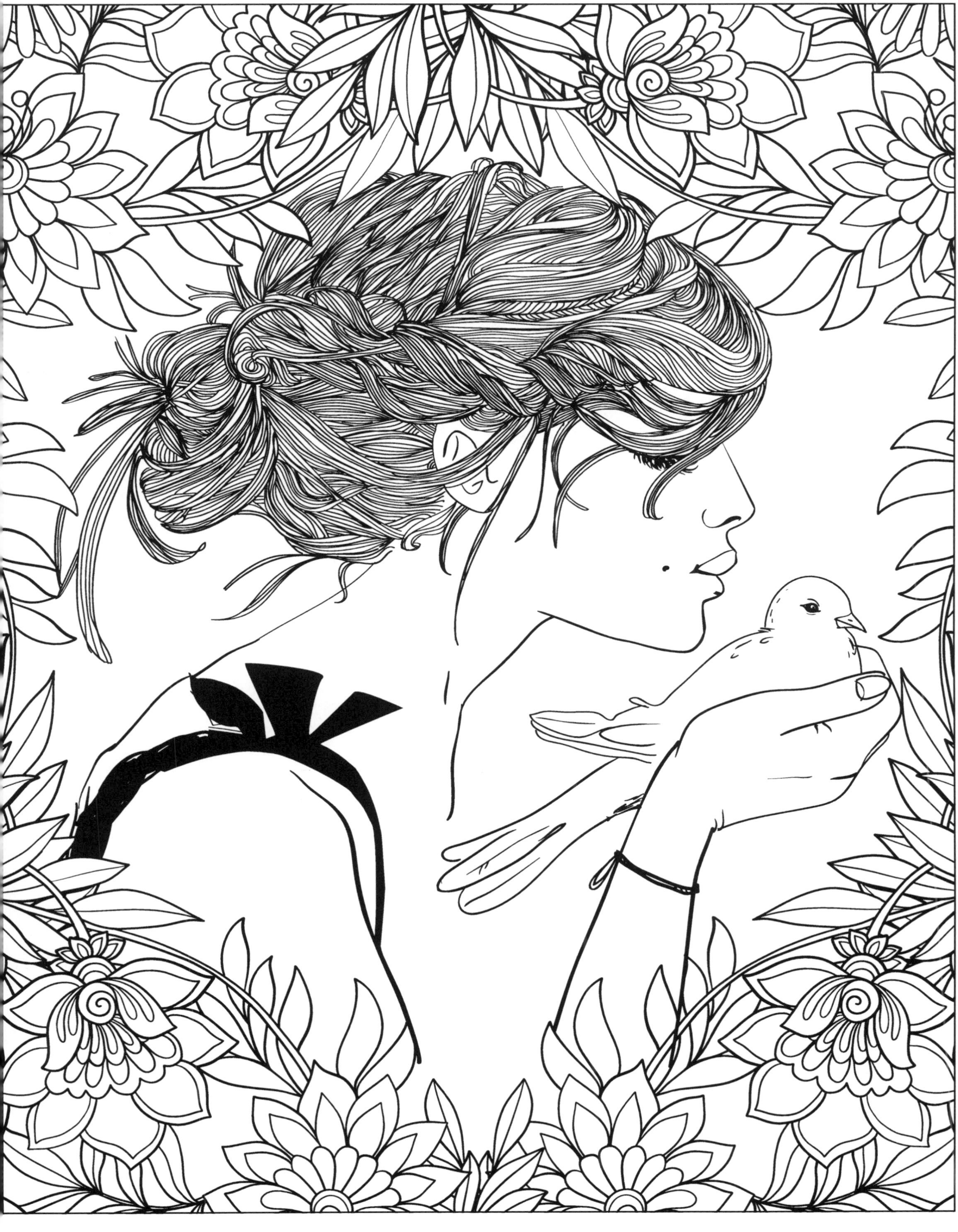

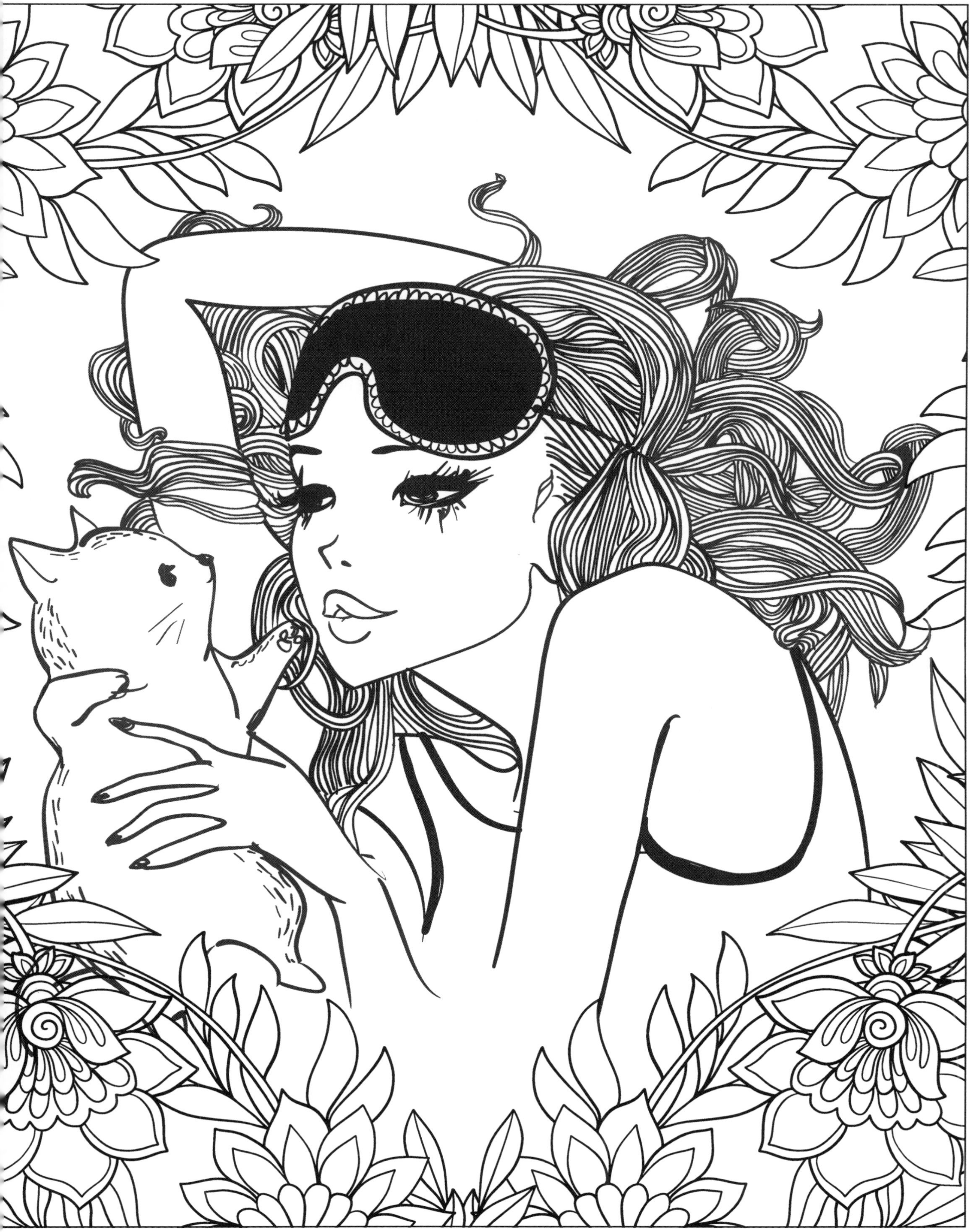

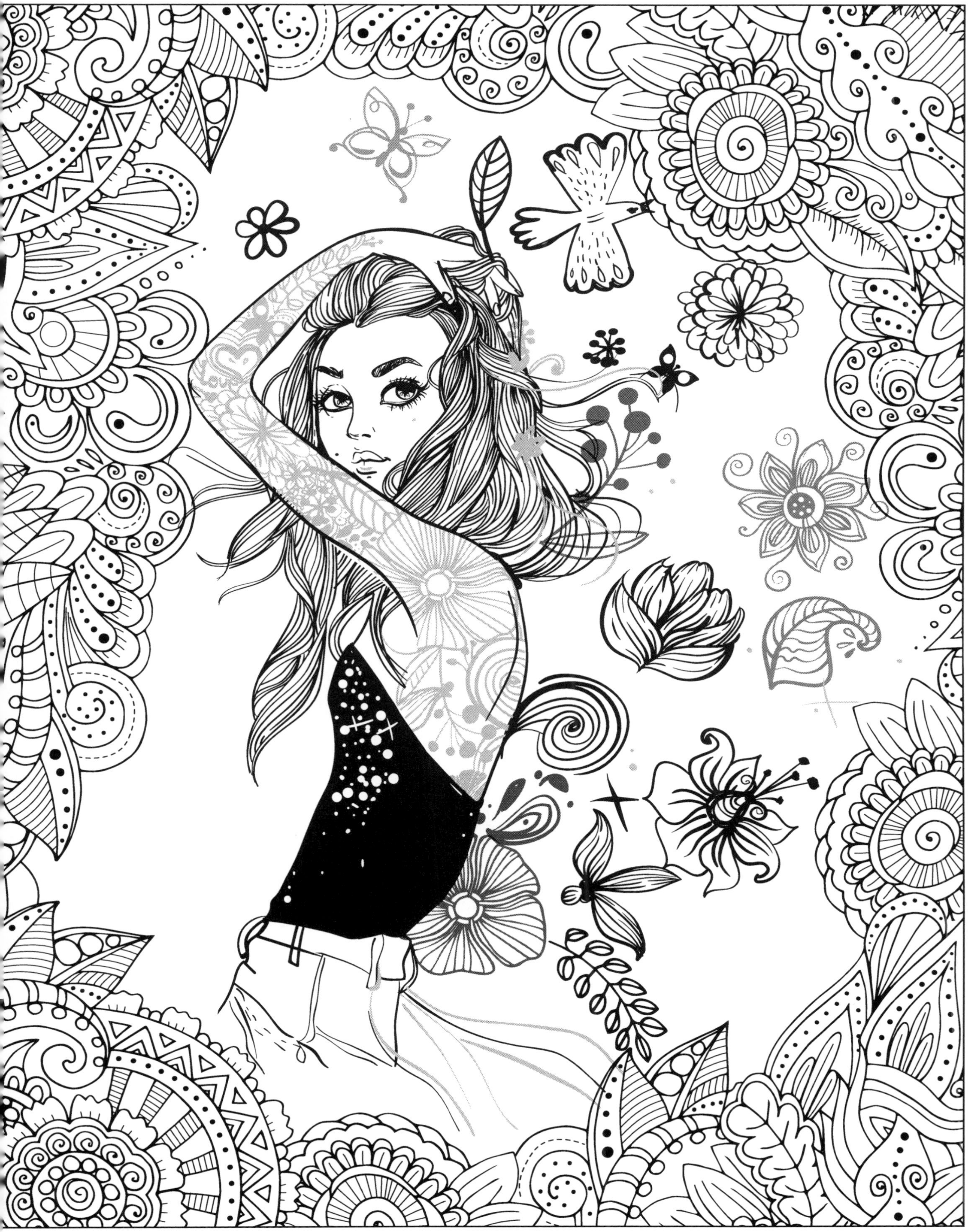

Printed in Great Britain
by Amazon

64054506R00056